THE
CHICKEN
GOURMET

THE
CHICKEN
GOURMET

TEMPTING WAYS WITH A
CLASSIC INGREDIENT

Linda Fraser

HERMES
HOUSE

First published in 1999 by Hermes House

© Anness Publishing Limited 1999

Hermes House is an imprint of Anness Publishing Limited
Hermes House, 88–89 Blackfriars Road, London SE1 8HA

A CIP catalogue record for this book is available from the British Library.

Publisher: Joanna Lorenz
Cookery Editors: Rosemary Wilkinson, Linda Doeser
Copy Editor: Rosie Hankin
Designer: Bill Mason
Illustrations: Anna Koska

Front cover: Lisa Tai, Designer; Thomas Odulate, Photographer; Helen Trent, Stylist;
Joy Skipper, Home Economist

Recipes: Catherine Atkinson, Alex Barker, Carla Capalbo, Maxine Clark, Andi Clevely, Christine France,
Sarah Gates, Shirley Gill, Carole Handslip, Norma MacMillan, Sue Maggs, Katherine Richmond,
Jenny Stacey, Ruby Le Bois, Liz Trigg, Hilaire Walden, Laura Washburn, Steven Wheeler
Photographers: Karl Adamson, Edward Allwright, Steve Baxter, James Duncan, John Freeman,
Michelle Garrett, Amanda Heywood, Don Last
Stylists: Madeleine Brehaut, Hilary Guy, Blake Minton, Kirsty Rawlings, Fiona Tillett
Food for Photography: Marilyn Forbes, Carole Handslip, Jane Hartshorn, Cara Hobday, Beverly LeBlanc,
Wendy Lee, Lucie McKelvie, Jenny Shapter, Elizabeth Silver, Jane Stevenson, Liz Trigg,
Elizabeth Wolf-Cohen

Previously published as part of a larger compendium, *Best-Ever Chicken*

Printed in Hong Kong/China

1 3 5 7 9 10 8 6 4 2

NOTES
For all recipes, quantities are given in both metric and imperial measures, and, where appropriate,
measures are also given in standard cups and spoons. Follow one set, but not a mixture, because they are
not interchangeable.

Standard spoon and cup measurements are level.
1 tsp = 5ml; 1 tbsp = 15ml; 1 cup = 250ml/8fl oz

Australian standard tablespoons are 20ml. Australian readers should use 3 tsp in place of 1 tbsp for
measuring small quantities of gelatine, cornflour, salt etc.

Medium eggs should be used unless otherwise stated.

CONTENTS

~

Introduction

Chicken has always been special and many of the great chefs of the past created their finest recipes around it. This superb collection includes many of these famous classics, as well as recipes inspired by cuisines from around the world and some exciting innovatory dishes. Whether you choose Coq au Vin, Blackened Cajun Chicken and Corn, or Chicken with Blackberries and Lemon, you can be sure that your taste buds are in for a treat.

❧

Chicken is wonderfully versatile, combining well with a vast range of other ingredients, herbs and spices. It can be cooked whole, cut into quarters, portions and joints, prepared as fillets, diced, sliced or even minced. It is suitable for every kind of cooking technique – from casseroles to barbecues and from pies to stir-fries. Many types of chicken are available in a wide variety of weights, including baby chickens, called poussins, which are just right for one or two servings. Chicken also has the advantage of being fairly inexpensive. An information-packed introduction to this book provides advice and clear step-by-step instructions for jointing, boning and spatchcocking chicken, as well as a variety of cooking techniques.

❧

Whatever the occasion, from a formal dinner party to Sunday lunch with the family, you will be sure to find a recipe for a chicken dish that will turn any meal into a gourmet treat.

Jointing Poultry

Although chickens and other poultry are sold already jointed into halves, quarters, breasts, thighs and drumsticks, sometimes it makes sense to buy a whole bird and to do the job yourself. That way you can prepare four larger pieces or eight smaller ones, depending on the recipe, and you can cut the pieces so the backbone and other bony bits (which can be saved for stock) are not included. In addition, a whole bird is cheaper to buy than pieces.

A sharp knife and sturdy kitchen scissors or poultry shears make the job of jointing poultry very easy.

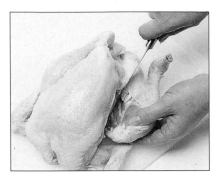

1 With the sharp knife, cut through the skin on one side of the body down to where the thigh joins the body. Bend the leg out away from the body and twist it to break the ball and socket joint.

2 Hold the leg out away from the body and cut through the ball and socket joint, taking the "oyster meat" from the backbone with the leg. Repeat on the other side.

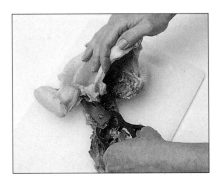

3 To separate the breast from the back, cut through the flap of skin just below the rib cage, cutting towards the neck. Pull the breast and back apart, cutting through the joints that connect them. Reserve the back for stock.

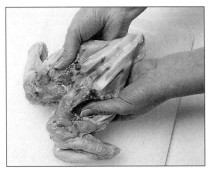

4 Turn the whole breast over, skin side down. Take one side of the breast in each hand and bend back firmly so the breastbone pops free. Loosen the bone on both sides with your fingers and using a knife to help, remove it.

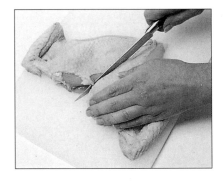

5 Cut the breast lengthways in half, cutting through the wishbone. You now have 2 breasts with wings attached and 2 leg portions.

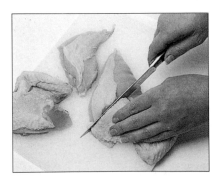

6 For 8 pieces, cut each breast in half at an angle so that some breast is included with each wing. Trim off any protruding bones.

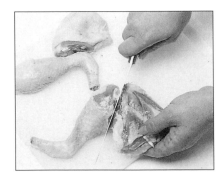

7 With the knife, cut each leg portion through the ball and socket joint to separate the thigh and drumstick.

TERMS FOR CHICKEN BREASTS

If the wing is left attached to the chicken breast, this is termed a "supreme". If the breast is completely boned, it is called a "fillet".

Boning a Chicken

For the purpose of stuffing and to make carving simple, it is essential to bone a chicken. Use a sharp knife with a short blade. Work in short, scraping movements, keeping the knife against the bone at all times, to leave the carcass clean.

This is a fiddly job, so allow yourself plenty of time.

Save the chicken bones, which will be ideal for making chicken stock.

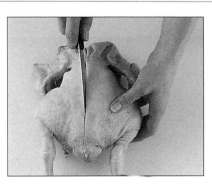

1 Remove any trussing string. Cut off the wing tips (pinions) and discard. With a short-bladed, sharp knife cut the skin along the underside (backbone) of the chicken. Carefully work the skin and flesh away from the carcass with the knife until the leg joints are exposed.

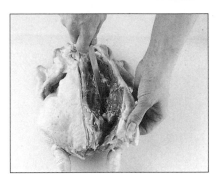

2 Cut the sinew between the ball and socket joints. This sinew joins the thigh bones and wings to the carcass.

3 Holding the rib cage away from the chicken body, carefully scrape the breastbone clean and cut the carcass away from the skin. Take great care not to cut through the skin, or the stuffing will burst out of the hole.

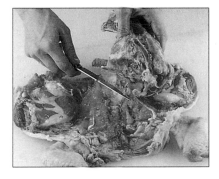

4 Take hold of the thigh bone in one hand, and with the knife scrape the flesh down the bone to the next joint.

5 Cut around the joint and continue cleaning the drumstick until the whole leg bone is free. Repeat with the other leg and both the wings. Lay the chicken flat and turn the flesh of the legs and wings inside the chicken. Flatten the flesh neatly ready for stuffing.

HANDLING RAW POULTRY

Raw poultry may harbour harmful organisms, such as salmonella bacteria, so it is vital to take care in its preparation. Always wash your hands, chopping board, knife and poultry shears in hot soapy water before and after handling poultry. If possible use a chopping board that can be washed at high temperature in a dishwasher and always keep a chopping board just for the preparation of raw poultry. Thaw frozen poultry completely before cooking.

Spatchcocking Poultry

Whole chickens, poussins, guinea fowl and game birds can be split in half and opened up flat like a book, to resemble the wings of a butterfly. They will then cook evenly under the grill or on a barbecue. A heavy chef's knife can be used to split the bird, but sturdy kitchen scissors or poultry shears are easier to handle.

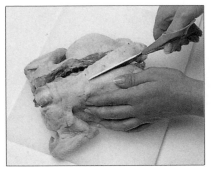

1 Set the bird breast down. Cut through the skin and rib cage along one side of the backbone, working from the tail end to the neck. Repeat on the other side of the backbone to cut it free. Keep the backbone for stock, if wished.

2 Turn the bird breast up. With the heel of your hand, press firmly on the breastbone to break it and flatten the breast.

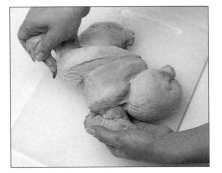

3 Fold the wing tips back behind the shoulders. Thread a long metal skewer through one wing and the top of the breast and out through the other wing.

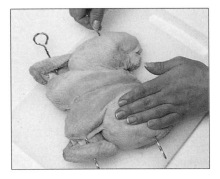

4 Thread a second skewer through the thighs and bottom of the breast. These skewers will keep the bird flat during cooking, and will make it easy to turn over.

TESTING POULTRY

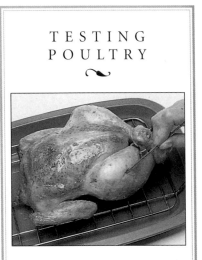

Overcooked poultry is dry, tough and tasteless, so knowing when a bird is done is crucial. The most reliable test for a whole bird is to insert a meat thermometer deep into the thigh meat (the internal temperature should be 79°C/175°F). Without a thermometer, you can test by piercing the thigh with a skewer or the tip of a knife; the juices that run out should be clear, not pink. Or lift the bird with a long two-pronged fork and tilt it so you can check the colour of the juices that run out of the cavity into the roasting tin. Pieces of poultry, particularly breasts, can be tested by pressing them with a finger; the meat should be firm but still slightly springy.

GRILLING TIMES FOR POULTRY

Note: Cook 10–15cm/4–6in from the heat; thinner pieces, less than 2.5cm/1in nearer the heat. If the poultry seems to be browning too quickly, turn down the heat slightly.

POUSSIN, SPATCHCOCKED	20–25 minutes
SPRING CHICKEN, SPLIT IN HALF OR SPATCHCOCKED	25–30 minutes
ROASTING CHICKEN, SPLIT IN HALF OR SPATCHCOCKED	30–40 minutes
CHICKEN BREAST, DRUMSTICK, THIGH	30–35 minutes
SKINLESS BONELESS CHICKEN BREAST	10–12 minutes
BONELESS DUCK BREAST	10–12 minutes

Frying Chicken

Fried chicken is justifiably popular – crisp and brown outside and tender and juicy within. It's a quick and easy cooking method that can be applied to pieces of rabbit and hare and small turkey joints, too.

Dry the pieces thoroughly with kitchen paper before frying. If they are at all wet, they will not brown properly. If the recipe directs, lightly coat the pieces with egg and crumbs or with a batter.

1 To pan-fry, heat oil, a mixture of oil and butter, or clarified butter in a large, heavy-based frying pan over moderate heat. When very hot, add the chicken pieces, skin-side down.

2 Fry until deep golden brown all over, turning the pieces during cooking. Fry until the pieces are thoroughly cooked. Remove pieces of breast before drumsticks and thighs. Drain on kitchen paper.

SUCCULENT FRIED CHICKEN
∽

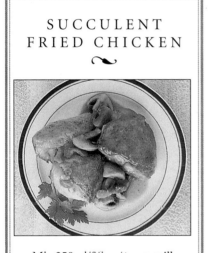

Mix 250ml/8fl oz/1 cup milk with 1 beaten egg in a shallow dish. On a sheet of greaseproof paper combine 150g/5oz/1¹/4 cups plain flour, 5ml/1 tsp paprika, and some salt and pepper. One at a time, dip eight chicken pieces in the egg mixture and turn them to coat all over. Then dip in the seasoned flour and shake off any excess. Deep-fry for 25–30 minutes, turning the pieces so they brown and cook evenly. Drain on kitchen paper and serve very hot.
Serves 4.

3 To deep-fry, dip the pieces into a mixture of milk and beaten egg and coat lightly with seasoned flour. Allow coating to set for 20 minutes before frying. (Or dip them in batter just before frying.)

4 Half fill a deep pan with vegetable oil. Heat it to 185°C/365°F. You can test the temperature with a cube of bread; if it takes 50 seconds to brown, the oil is at the right temperature.

5 With a fish slice or tongs, lower the chicken pieces into the oil, a few at a time. Deep-fry, turning during cooking, until they are golden brown all over and cooked.

6 Drain on kitchen paper and serve hot. If you want to keep a batch of fried chicken hot whilst frying the rest, put it, uncovered, into a low oven.

Making Poultry Sautés

A sauté combines frying and braising, producing particularly succulent results. It is a method suitable for pieces of poultry as well as for small whole birds such as quails and poussins.

As with frying, the poultry should be dried thoroughly with kitchen paper before cooking, to ensure that it browns quickly and evenly.

1 Heat a little oil, a mixture of oil and butter, or clarified butter in a heavy frying pan or sauté pan.

2 Add the poultry and fry over moderate heat until it is golden brown, turning to colour evenly.

3 Add any liquid and flavourings called for in the recipe. Bring to the boil, then cover and reduce the heat to moderately low. Continue cooking gently until the poultry is done, turning the pieces or birds over once or twice.

4 If the recipe instructs, remove the poultry from the pan and keep it warm while finishing the sauce. This can be as simple as boiling the cooking juices to reduce them or adding butter or cream for a richer result.

5 To thicken the cooking juices use equal weights of butter and flour mashed together. Use 25g/1oz of this "beurre manié" to 250ml/8fl oz/1 cup liquid. Add small pieces gradually to the hot juices and whisk until smooth.

6 Another method of thickening cooking juices is to use cornflour. Blend 10ml/2 tsp cornflour with 15ml/1 tbsp water and add to 250ml/8fl oz/1 cup juices. Boil, whisking, for 2–3 minutes, until the sauce is syrupy.

COUNTRY CHICKEN SAUTE

Cook 175g/6oz chopped bacon in 10ml/2 tsp oil over a moderately high heat until lightly coloured. Remove and reserve. Dredge a 1.5kg/3¹/₂lb chicken, cut into eight pieces, in seasoned flour. Fry in the bacon fat until evenly browned. Add 45ml/3 tbsp dry white wine and 250ml/8fl oz/1 cup poultry stock. Bring to the boil and add 225g/8oz quartered mushrooms sautéed in 15ml/1 tbsp of butter and the reserved bacon. Cover and cook over low heat for 20–25 minutes, or until the chicken is tender.
Serves 4.

Poaching, Casseroling & Braising

SIMPLE CHICKEN STOCK

This all-purpose chicken stock may be used as the basis for a wonderful home-made soup.

1 Put the giblets (the neck, gizzard and heart, but not the liver, as this makes stock bitter), or the carcass from a cooked chicken, into a pan and just cover with cold water.

2 Add a quartered onion, carrot, bouquet garni (bay leaf, thyme and parsley) and a few peppercorns. Bring to the boil, cover and simmer gently for 1–2 hours.

3 Remove any scum that rises to the surface with a slotted draining spoon. Alternatively, make the stock when you cook the chicken, by putting the giblets in the roasting tin around the chicken with the onion and herbs and just enough water to stop them from burning.

4 When the stock has set, carefully remove the fat from the surface with a spoon. Add salt to taste when using the stock.

POACHING

Poaching is a very gentle cooking method and produces stock for making a sauce afterwards.

1 Put the chicken into a flameproof casserole with a bouquet garni (bay leaf, thyme and parsley), carrot and onion.

2 Cover with water and add salt and peppercorns. Bring to the boil, cover and simmer for about 1¹⁄₂ hours or until tender.

3 Cool in the liquid or lift out, shred, and combine with a white sauce.

BRAISING

This method can be used for whole chickens and pieces and is ideal for strongly-flavoured meat.

1 Heat olive oil in a flameproof casserole and lightly fry a chicken or joints until golden.

2 Remove the chicken and fry 450g/1lb of diced vegetables (carrots, onions, celery and turnips), until soft.

3 Replace the chicken, cover tightly and cook very slowly on the hob or in a preheated oven at 160°C/325°F/Gas 3, until tender.

CASSEROLING

This slow-cooking method is good for large chicken joints with bones, or more mature meat.

1 Heat olive oil in a flameproof casserole and brown the chicken joints.

2 Add some stock, wine or a mixture of both to a depth of 2.5cm/1in. Add seasonings and herbs, cover, and cook on the hob or in the oven as for braising for 1–1¹⁄₂ hours or until tender.

3 Add a selection of lightly-fried vegetables such as baby onions, mushrooms, carrots and small new potatoes about halfway through the cooking time.

STARTERS

~

Sweet-spiced Chicken

Make sure you allow plenty of time for the chicken wings to marinate so the flavours develop well, then use a wok or a large frying pan for stir-frying.

INGREDIENTS

Serves 4

1 red chilli, finely chopped

5ml/1 tsp chilli powder

5ml/1 tsp ground ginger

rind of 1 lime, finely grated

12 chicken wings

60ml/2fl oz/^{1}/$_4$ cup sunflower oil

15ml/1 tbsp fresh coriander, chopped

30ml/2 tbsp soy sauce

50ml/3^1/$_2$ tbsp clear honey

lime rind and fresh coriander sprigs, to garnish

1 Mix the fresh chilli, chilli powder, ground ginger and lime rind together. Rub the mixture into the chicken skins and leave for at least 2 hours to allow the flavours to penetrate.

2 Heat a wok or large frying pan and add half of the oil. When the oil is hot, add half the wings and stir-fry for 10 minutes, turning regularly until crisp and golden. Drain on kitchen paper. Repeat with the remaining wings.

3 Add the coriander to the hot wok and stir-fry for 30 seconds, then return the wings to the wok and stir-fry for 1 minute.

4 Stir in the soy sauce and honey, and stir-fry for 1 minute. Serve the chicken wings hot with the sauce drizzled over them, garnished with lime rind and coriander sprigs.

San Francisco Chicken Wings

Make these as spicy as you like – just add more chilli sauce.

INGREDIENTS

Serves 4

85ml/3fl oz/³/4 cup soy sauce

15ml/1 tbsp light brown sugar

15ml/1 tbsp rice vinegar

30ml/2 tbsp dry sherry

juice of 1 orange

5cm/2in strip orange rind

1 star anise

5ml/1 tsp cornflour

50ml/2fl oz/¹/4 cup water

15ml/1 tbsp minced fresh root ginger

1.5–5ml/¹/4–1 tsp Oriental chilli-garlic
   sauce, to taste

1.5kg/3–3¹/2lb chicken wings, about
   22–24, tips removed

1 Preheat the oven to 200°C/ 400°F/Gas 6. Combine the ingredients for the sauce: the soy sauce, light brown sugar, rice vinegar, dry sherry, orange juice and rind and star anise, in a saucepan. Bring to the boil over a medium heat.

2 Combine the cornflour and water in a small bowl and stir until blended. Add to the boiling soy sauce mixture, stirring well. Boil for a further 1 minute, stirring all the time.

3 Remove the soy sauce mixture from the heat and stir in the minced ginger and chilli-garlic sauce to taste.

4 Arrange the chicken wings, in one layer, in a large baking dish. Pour over the soy sauce mixture and stir to coat the wings evenly.

5 Bake until tender and browned, 30–40 minutes, basting occasionally. Serve the wings hot or warm.

Chicken and Avocado Mayonnaise

You need quite firm scoops or forks to eat this starter, so don't be tempted to try to pass it round as a finger food.

INGREDIENTS

Serves 4

30ml/2 tbsp mayonnaise

15ml/1 tbsp fromage frais

2 garlic cloves, crushed

115g/4oz/1 cup chopped cooked chicken

1 large ripe, but firm, avocado, peeled and stoned

30ml/2 tbsp lemon juice

salt and black pepper

nacho chips or tortilla chips, to serve

1 Mix together the mayonnaise, fromage frais, garlic, and seasoning to taste, in a small bowl. Stir in the chopped chicken.

COOK'S TIP

This mixture also makes a great, chunky filling for sandwiches, baps or pitta bread. Or serve as a main course salad, heaped on to a base of mixed salad leaves.

2 Chop the avocado and toss immediately in lemon juice.

3 Mix the avocado gently into the chicken mixture. Check the seasoning and chill until required.

4 Serve in small serving dishes with the nacho or tortilla chips as scoops, if liked.

Chicken, Bacon and Walnut Terrine

To seal the terrine in the tin for longer storage, pour on melted lard.

INGREDIENTS

Serves 8–10

2 boneless chicken breasts

1 large garlic clove, crushed

1/2 slice bread

1 egg

350g/12oz bacon chops (the fattier the better), minced or finely chopped

225g/8oz chicken or turkey livers, finely chopped

25g/1oz/1/4 cup chopped walnuts, toasted

30ml/2 tbsp sweet sherry or Madeira

2.5ml/1/2 tsp ground allspice

2.5ml/1/2 tsp cayenne pepper

pinch each ground nutmeg and cloves

8 long rashers streaky bacon, rind removed

salt and black pepper

chicory leaves and chives, to garnish

1 Cut the chicken breasts into thin strips and season lightly. Mash the garlic, bread and egg together. Work in the chopped bacon (using your hands is really the best way) and then the finely chopped livers. Stir in the chopped walnuts, sherry or Madeira, spices and seasoning to taste.

2 Preheat the oven to 200°C/ 400°F/Gas 6. Stretch each of the bacon rashers with a palette knife and use to line a 675g/1 1/2lb loaf tin, then pack in half of the meat mixture.

3 Lay the chicken strips on the top and spread the rest of the mixture over. Cover the loaf tin with lightly-greased foil, seal well and press down very firmly.

4 Place the terrine in a roasting tin half-full of hot water and bake for 1–1 1/2 hours, or until firm to the touch. Remove from the oven, place weights on the top and leave to cool completely. Drain off any excess fat or liquid while the terrine is warm.

5 When really cold, turn out the terrine, cut into thick slices and serve at once, garnished with a few chicory leaves and chives.

Brandied Chicken Liver Pâté

The rich flavour of chicken livers in this delicious starter is enhanced by the addition of a little brandy.

INGREDIENTS

Serves 4–6

350g/12oz chicken livers

115g/4oz/½ cup butter

1 rindless streaky bacon slice, chopped

1 shallot, chopped

2 garlic cloves, crushed

30ml/2 tbsp brandy

30ml/2 tbsp chopped fresh parsley

salt and freshly ground black pepper

fresh bay leaves and peppercorns,
   to garnish

olive bread, to serve

1 Rinse, trim and roughly chop the chicken livers. Melt half the butter in a large, heavy-based frying pan. Add the chopped bacon, shallot and garlic and fry over a medium heat for 5 minutes. Add the chicken livers and fry gently, stirring occasionally, for a further 5 minutes.

COOK'S TIP

If the pâté is properly sealed with melted butter poured over the entire surface, it will keep in the refrigerator for 3–4 days. It can, therefore, be prepared in advance for a dinner party.

2 Stir in the brandy and parsley and season with salt and pepper. Bring to the boil and cook for about 2 minutes, then remove from the heat and process in a food processor until smooth.

3 Spoon the pâté into individual dishes and smooth the surface. Heat the remaining butter until it has just melted, but do not allow it to turn brown. Pour it carefully over the surface of each dish of pâté to seal. Garnish with bay leaves and peppercorns. Set aside to cool completely.

4 When cool, chill the pâté in the refrigerator until firm. Serve with olive bread.

Pan-fried Chicken Liver Salad

This Florentine salad uses vin santo, a sweet dessert wine from Tuscany, but this is not essential – any dessert wine will do. Alternatively, you could use a sweet or cream sherry.

INGREDIENTS

Serves 4

75g/3oz fresh baby spinach leaves

75g/3oz lollo rosso or lollo biondo leaves

75ml/5 tbsp olive oil

15g/½oz/1 tbsp butter

225g/8oz chicken livers, trimmed and thinly sliced

45ml/3 tbsp vin santo

50–75g/2–3oz fresh Parmesan cheese, shaved into curls

salt and freshly ground black pepper

1 Separate the spinach and lollo rosso or lollo biondo leaves, then wash and thoroughly dry them. Tear the leaves into fairly small pieces and place them in a large bowl. Season with salt and pepper to taste and toss gently to mix.

2 Heat 30ml/2 tbsp of the oil with the butter in a large frying pan. When foaming, add the chicken livers and stir over a medium heat for 5 minutes, or until the livers are browned on the outside, but still pink in the centre. Remove from the heat.

3 Remove the livers from the pan, drain them on kitchen paper, then place on top of the spinach.

4 Return the pan to the heat, add the remaining oil and the wine and stir until sizzling. Pour the hot dressing over the salad, toss to mix, transfer to a serving dish and garnish with the cheese.

Spicy Chicken Canapés

*These tiny little cocktail sandwiches
have a spicy filling, and are finished
with different toppings. Use square
bread so that you can cut out more
rounds and have less wastage.*

INGREDIENTS

Makes 18

75g/3oz/³/4 cup finely chopped
   cooked chicken

2 spring onions, finely chopped

30ml/2 tbsp chopped red pepper

90ml/6 tbsp curry mayonnaise

6 slices white bread

15ml/1 tbsp paprika

15ml/1 tbsp chopped fresh parsley

30ml/2 tbsp chopped salted
   peanuts

2 Spread the spring onion and
red pepper mixture over three
of the bread slices and sandwich
with the remaining bread,
pressing well together. Spread the
remaining curry mayonnaise over
the top and cut into 4cm/1½in
circles using a plain cutter.

3 Dip into paprika, chopped
parsley or chopped nuts and
arrange attractively on a plate.

1 In a bowl, mix the chopped
chicken with the chopped
spring onions, red pepper and half
the curry mayonnaise.

Chicken Cigars

These small crispy rolls can be served warm as canapés with a drink before a meal, or as a first course with a crisp, colourful salad.

INGREDIENTS

Serves 4

275g/10oz packet of filo pastry

45ml/3 tbsp olive oil

fresh parsley, to garnish

For the filling

350g/12oz/3 cups minced raw chicken

salt and freshly ground black pepper

1 egg, beaten

2.5ml/$\frac{1}{2}$ tsp ground cinnamon

2.5ml/$\frac{1}{2}$ tsp ground ginger

30ml/2 tbsp raisins

15ml/1 tbsp olive oil

1 small onion, finely chopped

1 Mix all the filling ingredients, except the oil and onion, together in a bowl. Heat the oil in a large frying pan and cook the onion until tender. Leave to cool. Add the mixed filling ingredients.

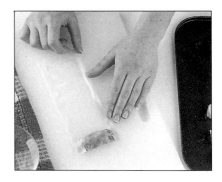

2 Preheat the oven to 180°C/ 350°F/Gas 4. Once the filo pastry packet has been opened, keep the pastry covered at all times with a damp dish towel. Work fast, as the pastry dries out very quickly when exposed to the air. Unravel the pastry and cut into 25 x 10cm/ 10 x 4in strips.

3 Take a strip (cover the remainder), brush with a little oil and place a small spoonful of filling about 1cm/$\frac{1}{2}$in from the end.

4 To encase the filling, fold the sides inwards to a width of 5cm/2in and roll into a cigar shape. Place on a greased baking sheet and brush with oil. Repeat to use all the filling. Bake for about 20–25 minutes until golden brown and crisp. Garnish with fresh parsley and serve.

Chicken Roulades

These chicken rolls make a light lunch dish for two, or a starter for four. They can be sliced and served cold with a salad.

INGREDIENTS

Makes 4

4 chicken thighs, boned and skinned

115g/4oz chopped fresh or frozen spinach

15g/^{1}/2oz/1 tbsp butter

25g/1oz/2 tbsp pine nuts

pinch of grated nutmeg

25g/1oz/7 tbsp fresh white breadcrumbs

4 rashers rindless streaky bacon

30ml/2 tbsp olive oil

150ml/^{1}/4 pint/^{2}/3 cup white wine
  or chicken stock

10ml/2 tsp cornflour

30ml/2 tbsp single cream

15ml/1 tbsp snipped fresh chives

salt and black pepper

1 Preheat the oven to 180°C/ 350°F/Gas 4. Place the chicken thighs between clear film and flatten with a rolling pin.

2 Put the spinach and butter into a saucepan, heat gently until the spinach has defrosted, if frozen, then increase the heat and cook rapidly, stirring occasionally until all the moisture has been driven off. Add the pine nuts, seasoning, nutmeg and fresh breadcrumbs.

3 Divide the filling between the chicken pieces and roll up neatly. Wrap a rasher of bacon around each piece and tie securely with fine string.

4 Heat the oil in a large frying pan and brown the rolls all over. Lift out using a slotted spoon to drain off the oil and place in a shallow ovenproof dish.

5 Pour over the wine or stock, cover, and bake for 15–20 minutes, or until tender. Transfer the chicken to a serving plate and remove the string. Strain the cooking liquid into a saucepan.

6 Blend the cornflour with a little cold water and add to the juices in the pan, along with the cream. Bring to the boil, stirring until thick. Adjust the seasoning and add the chives. Pour the sauce around the chicken and serve.

Warm Chicken and Coriander Salad

This salad needs to be served warm to make the most of the wonderful sesame and coriander flavourings. It makes a simple starter or a delicious light lunch dish.

INGREDIENTS

Serves 6

4 medium chicken breasts, boned and skinned

225g/8oz mange-touts

2 heads decorative lettuce such as lollo rosso or oakleaf

3 carrots, peeled and cut into small matchsticks

175g/6oz/2³/4 cups button mushrooms, sliced

6 rashers of bacon, fried and chopped

1 tbsp chopped fresh coriander leaves, to garnish

Dressing

120ml/4fl oz/¹/2 cup lemon juice

30ml/2 tbsp wholegrain mustard

250ml/8fl oz/1 cup olive oil

60ml/4 tbsp sesame oil

1 tsp coriander seeds, crushed

1 Mix all the dressing ingredients in a bowl. Place the chicken breasts in a shallow dish and pour on half the dressing. Chill overnight, and store the remaining dressing in the fridge.

2 Cook the mange-touts for 2 minutes in boiling water, then cool under running cold water to stop them cooking any further. Tear the lettuces into small pieces and mix the other salad ingredients and the bacon together. Arrange all these in individual serving dishes.

3 Grill the chicken breasts until cooked through, then slice them on the diagonal into quite thin pieces. Divide among the bowls of salad, and add some dressing to each dish. Combine quickly and scatter some fresh coriander over each bowl.

Corn-fed Chicken Salad

*A light first course for eight or a
substantial main course for four.*

INGREDIENTS

Serves 8

1.75kg/4lb corn-fed chicken

300ml/^{1}/$_2$ pint/1^1/$_4$ cups white wine
  and water, mixed

24 x 5mm/^{1}/$_4$ in slices French bread

1 garlic clove, peeled

225g/8oz French beans, trimmed and cut
  in 5cm/2in lengths

115g/4oz fresh young spinach leaves,
  washed and torn into small pieces

2 sticks celery, thinly sliced

2 sun-dried tomatoes, chopped

2 spring onions, thinly sliced

fresh chives and parsley, to garnish

For the vinaigrette

30ml/2 tbsp red wine vinegar

90ml/6 tbsp olive oil

15ml/1 tbsp wholegrain mustard

15ml/1 tbsp clear honey

30ml/2 tbsp chopped mixed fresh herbs

10ml/2 tsp finely chopped capers

salt and black pepper

2 Put all the ingredients for the
vinaigrette into a screw-topped
jar and shake vigorously. Adjust
the seasoning to taste.

3 Toast the French bread until
golden brown. Rub with garlic.

4 Cook the French beans in
boiling water until just tender.
Drain and rinse under cold water.

5 Arrange the spinach on serving
plates with the celery, French
beans, sun-dried tomatoes,
chicken and spring onions. Spoon
over the dressing, add the toasted
croûtes and garnish with chives
and parsley.

1 Preheat the oven to 190°C/
375°F/Gas 5. Put the chicken,
wine and water into a casserole.
Roast for 1^1/$_2$ hours until tender.
Leave to cool in the liquid. Remove
the skin and bones and cut the
flesh into small pieces.

ROASTS & BAKES

~

Galveston Chicken

*An American favourite, crisp
roasted chicken with garlic.*

Serves 4

1.5kg/3–3¹/₂lb chicken

juice of 1 lemon

4 garlic cloves, crushed

15ml/1 tbsp cayenne pepper

15ml/1 tbsp paprika

15ml/1 tbsp dried oregano

2.5ml/¹/₂ tsp coarse black pepper

10ml/2 tsp olive oil

5ml/1 tsp salt

1 With a sharp knife or poultry
shears, remove the backbone
from the chicken. Turn it breast
side up. With the heel of your
hand, press down to break the
breastbone, and open the chicken
flat like a book. Insert a skewer
through the chicken, at the thighs,
to keep it flat during cooking.

2 Place the chicken in a shallow
dish and pour over the lemon
juice to coat.

3 In a small bowl, combine the
garlic, cayenne, paprika,
oregano, pepper and oil. Mix well.
Rub evenly over the surface of the
chicken.

4 Cover and let marinate 2–3
hours at room temperature, or
chill overnight (return to room
temperature before roasting).

5 Season the chicken with salt on
both sides. Transfer it to a
shallow roasting pan.

6 Put the pan in a cold oven and
set the temperature to 200°C/
400°F/Gas 6. Roast until the
chicken is done, about 1 hour,
turning occasionally and basting
with the pan juices. To test, prick
with a skewer: the juices that run
out should be clear.

COOK'S TIP

Roasting chicken in an oven that
has not been preheated produces
a particularly crispy skin.

Roast Chicken with Celeriac

Chicken with a stuffing of celeriac, bacon, onion and herbs.

INGREDIENTS

Serves 4

1.6kg/3^1/2lb chicken

15g/^{1}/2oz/1 tbsp butter

For the stuffing

450g/1lb celeriac, chopped

25g/1oz/2 tbsp butter

3 slices bacon, chopped

1 onion, finely chopped

leaves from 1 thyme sprig, chopped

leaves from 1 small tarragon
    sprig, chopped

30ml/2 tbsp chopped fresh parsley

75g/3oz/1^1/2 cups fresh brown
    breadcrumbs

dash of Worcestershire sauce

1 egg

salt and pepper

1 To make the stuffing, cook the celeriac in boiling water until tender. Drain well and chop finely.

2 Heat the butter in a saucepan, then gently cook the bacon and onion until the onion is soft. Stir the celeriac and herbs into the pan and cook, stirring occasionally, for 2–3 minutes. Meanwhile, preheat the oven to 200°C/400°F/Gas 6.

3 Remove the pan from the heat and stir in the fresh bread-crumbs, Worcestershire sauce, seasoning and sufficient egg to bind.

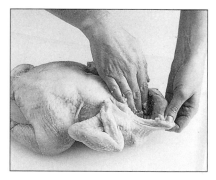

4 Place the stuffing in the neck end of the chicken. Season the bird's skin, then rub with the butter. Roast the chicken, basting occasionally with the juices, for 1^1/4–1^1/2 hours, until the juices run clear when the thickest part of the leg is pierced. Rest for 10 minutes in a warm place before carving.

Moroccan Harissa-spiced Roast Chicken

Roast chicken with a difference – the spices and fruit in the stuffing impart a delicious flavour to the chicken, while also helping to keep it moist.

Serves 4–5

1.5kg/3–3½lb chicken
30–60ml/2–4 tbsp garlic and spice
   aromatic oil
a few bay leaves
10ml/2 tsp clear honey
10ml/2 tsp tomato purée
60ml/4 tbsp lemon juice
150ml/¼ pint/⅔ cup chicken stock
2.5–5ml/½–1 tsp harissa

For the stuffing

25g/1oz/2 tbsp butter
1 onion, chopped
1 garlic clove, crushed
7.5ml/1½ tsp ground cinnamon
2.5ml/½ tsp ground cumin
225g/8oz/1⅓ cups dried fruit, soaked in
   water for several hours or overnight
25g/1oz/¼ cup blanched almonds,
   finely chopped
salt and freshly ground black pepper

1 First make the stuffing. Melt the butter in a saucepan over a low heat. Add the onion and garlic and cook gently, stirring frequently, for 5 minutes, or until the onion is soft and translucent. Add the ground cinnamon and cumin and cook, stirring constantly, for 2 minutes.

2 Drain the dried fruit and discard the soaking water. Roughly chop the fruit and add it to the stuffing, together with the almonds. Season with salt and pepper and cook, stirring constantly, for a further 2 minutes. Tip the stuffing into a bowl and set aside to cool.

3 Preheat the oven to 200°C/400°F/Gas 6. Stuff the neck of the chicken with the fruit mixture, reserving any excess. Place the chicken in a roasting tin and tuck in the bay leaves, then brush with the garlic and spice oil. Cook for 1–1¼ hours, basting occasionally with the juices, until cooked.

4 Remove the chicken from the tin and pour off any excess fat. Stir the honey, tomato purée, lemon juice, stock and harissa into the juices and season. Bring to the boil and simmer, stirring, for 2 minutes. Reheat any extra stuffing. Carve the chicken, and serve with the sauce and stuffing.

Poussins with Bulgur Wheat and Vermouth

Vermouth is a valuable asset in the kitchen. It appears twice in this recipe, first flavouring the bulgur wheat stuffing and then in the glaze for the poussins.

INGREDIENTS

Serves 4

50g/2oz/⅓ cup bulgur wheat
150ml/¼ pint/⅔ cup dry white vermouth
60ml/4 tbsp olive oil
1 large onion, finely chopped
2 carrots, finely chopped
75g/3oz/1 cup pine nuts, chopped
5ml/1 tsp celery seeds
4 poussins
3 red onions, quartered
4 baby aubergines, halved
4 patty pan squashes
12 baby carrots
45ml/3 tbsp corn syrup
salt and freshly ground black pepper

1 Preheat the oven to 200°C/400°F/Gas 6. Put the bulgur wheat in a heatproof bowl, pour over half the vermouth and cover with boiling water. Set aside.

2 Heat half the oil in a large frying pan. Fry the onion and carrots for 10 minutes, then remove the pan from the heat and stir in the pine nuts, celery seeds and well-drained bulgur wheat.

3 Stuff the poussins with the bulgur wheat mixture. Place them in a roasting tin, brush with oil and sprinkle with salt and pepper. Roast for 45–55 minutes, until cooked.

4 Meanwhile, spread out the red onion quarters, aubergine halves, patty pan squashes and baby carrots in a single layer on a baking sheet.

5 Mix together the corn syrup, the remaining vermouth and the remaining oil in a small bowl. Season with salt and pepper to taste. Brush the corn syrup mixture over the vegetables and roast for 35–45 minutes, until golden. Cut each poussin in half with a sharp knife and arrange them on warm individual serving plates with the roasted vegetables. Serve immediately.

Poussins with Raisin and Walnut Stuffing

Port wine-soaked raisins, walnuts and mushrooms make an unusual stuffing for poussins.

INGREDIENTS

Serves 4

250ml/8fl oz/1 cup Port wine

50g/2oz/⅓ cup raisins

15ml/1 tbsp walnut oil

75g/3oz mushrooms, minced

1 large celery stick, minced

1 small onion, chopped

salt and pepper

50g/2oz/1 cup fresh breadcrumbs

50g/2oz/½ cup chopped walnuts

15ml/1 tbsp each chopped fresh basil and
    parsley, or 30ml/2 tbsp chopped parsley

2.5ml/½ tsp dried thyme

75g/3oz/6 tbsp butter, melted

4 poussins

1 Preheat the oven to 180°C/ 350°F/Gas 4.

2 In a small bowl, combine the Port wine and raisins and leave to soak for about 20 minutes.

3 Meanwhile, heat the oil in a non-stick pan. Add the mushrooms, celery, onion and 1.5ml/¼ tsp salt and cook over a low heat until softened, about 8–10 minutes. Leave to cool.

4 Drain the raisins, reserving the Port. Combine the raisins, breadcrumbs, walnuts, basil, parsley and thyme in a bowl. Stir in the onion mixture and 50g/2oz/ 4 tbsp of the butter. Add 2.5ml/½ tsp salt and pepper to taste.

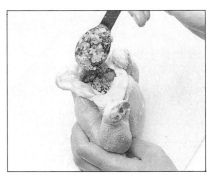

5 Fill the cavity of each poussin with the stuffing. Do not pack down. Tie the legs together, to enclose the stuffing securely.

6 Brush the poussins with the remaining butter and place in a baking dish just large enough to hold the birds comfortably. Pour over the reserved Port wine.

7 Roast, basting occasionally, for about 1 hour. Test by piercing the thigh with a skewer; the juices should run clear. Serve immediately with some of the juices.

Poussins with Dirty Rice

This rice is called dirty not because of the bits in it (though the roux and chicken livers do "muss" it up a bit) but because jazz is called "dirty music", and the rice in this recipe is certainly jazzed up.

INGREDIENTS

Serves 4

For the rice

60ml/4 tbsp cooking oil

25g/1oz/^{1}/4 cup plain flour

50g/2oz/4 tbsp butter

1 large onion, chopped

2 celery sticks, chopped

1 green pepper, seeded and diced

2 garlic cloves, crushed

200g/7oz minced pork

225g/8oz chicken livers, trimmed
   and sliced

Tabasco sauce

300ml/^{1}/2 pint/1^1/4 cups chicken stock

4 spring onions, shredded

45ml/3 tbsp chopped fresh parsley

225g/8oz/generous 1 cup American
   long-grain rice, cooked

salt and black pepper

For the birds

4 poussins

2 bay leaves, halved

25g/1oz/2 tbsp butter

1 lemon

COOK'S TIP
~

You can substitute quails for the poussins, in which case offer two per person and stuff each little bird with 10ml/2 tsp of the dirty rice before roasting for about 20 minutes.

---

1 In a small heavy-based saucepan, make a roux by blending together 2 tbsp of the oil and the flour. When it is a chestnut brown colour, remove the pan from the heat and place it immediately on a cold surface.

2 Heat the remaining 2 tbsp oil with the butter in a frying pan and stir-fry the onion, celery and green pepper for about 5 minutes.

3 Add the garlic and pork and stir-fry for about 5 minutes, breaking up the pork and stirring well to cook it all over.

4 Add the chicken livers and fry for 2–3 minutes until they have changed colour all over. Season with salt and black pepper and a dash of Tabasco sauce.

5 Stir the roux into the stir-fried mixture, then gradually add the stock. When it begins to bubble, cover and cook for 30 minutes, stirring occasionally. Uncover and cook for a further 15 minutes, stirring frequently.

6 Preheat the oven to 200°C/400°F/Gas 6. Mix the shredded spring onions and chopped parsley into the meat mixture and stir it all into the cooked rice.

7 Put ^{1}/2 bay leaf and 1 tbsp rice into each poussin. Rub the outside with the butter and season with salt and pepper.

8 Put the birds on a rack in a roasting tin, squeeze the juice from the lemon over them and roast in the oven for 35–40 minutes, basting twice during cooking with the pan juices.

9 Put the remaining rice into a shallow ovenproof dish, cover it and place on a low shelf in the oven for the last 15–20 minutes of the birds' cooking time.

10 Serve the birds on a bed of dirty rice with the roasting juices (drained of fat) poured over.

Poussins with Grapes in Vermouth

A rather special dish which is ideal to serve when entertaining.

Serves 4

4 oven-ready poussins, about
    450g/1lb each
50g/2oz/4 tbsp butter, softened
2 shallots, chopped
60ml/4 tbsp chopped fresh parsley
225g/8oz white grapes, preferably
    muscatel, halved and seeded
150ml/$^1/_4$ pint/$^2/_3$ cup white vermouth
5ml/1 tsp cornflour
60ml/4 tbsp double cream
30ml/2 tbsp pine nuts, toasted
salt and black pepper
watercress sprigs, to garnish

1 Preheat the oven to 200°C/
400°F/Gas 6. Spread the softened butter all over the poussins
and put a hazelnut-sized piece in
the cavity of each bird.

2 Mix together the shallots and
parsley and place a quarter of
the mixture inside each poussin.
Put the poussins side by side in a
large roasting tin and roast for
40–50 minutes, or until the juices
run clear when the thickest part of
the flesh is pierced with a skewer.
Put the poussins on to a warm
serving dish, cover and keep warm.

3 Skim off most of the fat from
the roasting tin, then add the
grapes and vermouth. Place the tin
directly over a low flame for a few
minutes to warm and slightly
soften the grapes.

4 Lift the grapes out of the tin
using a slotted spoon and
scatter them around the poussins.
Keep covered. Stir the cornflour
into the cream, then add to the pan
juices. Cook gently for a few
minutes, stirring, until the sauce
has thickened. Adjust seasoning.

5 Pour the sauce around the
poussins. Sprinkle with the
toasted pine nuts and garnish with
watercress sprigs.

Chicken Roll

The roll can be prepared and cooked the day before and will freeze well too. Remove from the fridge about an hour before serving.

INGREDIENTS

Serves 8

2kg/4¹/2lb chicken

For the stuffing

1 medium onion, finely chopped

50g/2oz/4 tbsp melted butter

350g/12oz/2 cups lean minced pork

115g/4oz streaky bacon, chopped

15ml/1 tbsp chopped fresh parsley

10ml/2 tsp chopped fresh thyme

115g/4oz/2 cups fresh white breadcrumbs

30ml/2 tbsp sherry

1 large egg, beaten

25g/1oz/¹/4 cup shelled pistachio nuts

25g/1oz/¹/4 cup stoned black olives
   (about 12)

salt and black pepper

1 To make the stuffing, cook the chopped onion gently in 25g/1oz/2 tbsp of the butter until soft. Turn into a bowl and cool. Add the remaining ingredients, mix thoroughly and season with salt and black pepper.

2 To bone the chicken, use a small, sharp knife to remove the wing tips. Turn the chicken on to its breast and cut a line down the backbone.

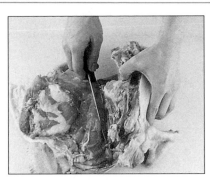

3 Cut the meat away from the carcass, scraping the bones clean. Carefully cut through the sinew around the leg and wing joints and scrape down the bones to free them. Remove the carcass, taking care not to cut through the skin along the breastbone.

4 To stuff the chicken, lay it flat, skin side down and flatten as much as possible. Shape the stuffing down the centre of the chicken and fold in the sides.

5 Sew the meat neatly together, using a needle and dark thread. Tie with fine string into a roll.

6 Preheat the oven to 180°C/ 350°F/Gas 4. Put the roll, join underneath, on a rack in a roasting tin and brush with the remaining butter. Cook, uncovered, for about 1¹/4 hours. Baste with the juices during cooking. Leave to cool. Remove the string and thread. Wrap in foil and chill until needed.

Parmesan Chicken Bake

The tomato sauce may be made the day before and left to cool. Serve with crusty bread and salad.

INGREDIENTS

Serves 4

4 chicken breasts, boned and skinned

60ml/4 tbsp plain flour

60ml/4 tbsp olive oil

salt and black pepper

For the tomato sauce

15ml/1 tbsp olive oil

1 onion, finely chopped

1 stick celery, finely chopped

1 red pepper, seeded and diced

1 garlic clove, crushed

400g/14oz can chopped tomatoes with the juice

150ml/$^1/_4$ pint/$^2/_3$ cup chicken stock

15ml/1 tbsp tomato purée

10ml/2 tsp caster sugar

15ml/1 tbsp chopped fresh basil

15ml/1 tbsp chopped fresh parsley

To assemble

225g/8oz mozzarella cheese, sliced

60ml/4 tbsp grated Parmesan cheese

30ml/2 tbsp fresh breadcrumbs

1 To make the tomato sauce, heat 15ml/1 tbsp of the oil in a frying pan and gently cook the onion, celery, pepper and crushed garlic in the oil until tender.

2 Add the tomatoes with their juice, the stock, purée, sugar and herbs. Season to taste and bring to the boil. Simmer for 30 minutes to make a thick sauce, stirring occasionally.

3 Divide the chicken breasts into two natural fillets, place between sheets of clear film and flatten to a thickness of 5mm/$^1/_4$in with a rolling pin.

4 Season the flour. Toss the chicken breasts in the flour to coat, shaking to remove the excess.

5 Preheat the oven to 180°C/350°F/Gas 4. Heat the remaining oil in a large frying pan and cook the chicken quickly in batches for 3–4 minutes until coloured. Remove and keep warm while frying the rest of the chicken.

6 To assemble, layer the chicken pieces in a large baking dish with the cheeses and thick tomato sauce, finishing with a layer of cheese and breadcrumbs on top. Bake uncovered for 20–30 minutes or until golden brown.

Tandoori Chicken

A famous Indian/Pakistani chicken dish which is cooked in a clay oven called a tandoor, this is extremely popular in the West and appears on the majority of the restaurant menus. Though the authentic tandoori flavour is very difficult to achieve in conventional ovens, this version still makes a very tasty dish.

INGREDIENTS

Serves 4

4 chicken quarters

175ml/6fl oz/³/₄ cup natural low-fat yogurt

5ml/1 tsp garam masala

5ml/1 tsp chopped fresh root ginger

5ml/1 tsp chopped garlic

7.5ml/1¹/₂ tsp chilli powder

1.5ml/¹/₄ tsp ground turmeric

5ml/1 tsp ground coriander

15ml/1 tbsp lemon juice

5ml/1 tsp salt

a few drops red food colouring

30ml/2 tbsp corn oil

To garnish

mixed salad leaves

lime wedges

1 tomato, quartered

2 Mix together the yogurt, garam masala, ginger, garlic, chilli powder, turmeric, ground coriander, lemon juice, salt, red food colouring and oil, and beat until well mixed together.

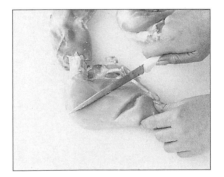

1 Skin, rinse and pat dry the chicken quarters. Make 2 slits into the flesh of each piece, place in a dish and set aside.

3 Cover the chicken quarters with the yogurt and spice mixture and leave to marinate for about 3 hours.

4 Preheat the oven to 240°C/475°F/Gas 9. Transfer the chicken pieces to an ovenproof dish.

5 Bake in the oven for 20–25 minutes, or until the chicken is cooked right through and browned on top.

6 Remove from the oven, transfer to a serving dish and garnish with the salad leaves, lime and tomato.

Chicken, Carrot and Leek Parcels

These intriguing parcels may sound a bit fiddly for everyday, but they take very little time and you can freeze them – ready to cook gently from frozen.

INGREDIENTS

Serves 4

4 chicken fillets or boneless breasts

2 small leeks, sliced

2 carrots, grated

4 stoned black olives, chopped

1 garlic clove, crushed

15–30ml/1–2 tbsp olive oil

8 anchovy fillets

salt and black pepper

black olives and herb sprigs, to garnish

1 Preheat the oven to 200°C/ 400°F/Gas 6. Season the chicken well with salt and pepper.

2 Divide the leeks equally among four sheets of greased grease-proof paper, about 23cm/9in square. Place a piece of chicken on top of each one.

3 Mix the carrots, olives, garlic and oil together. Season lightly and place on top of the chicken portions. Top each with two of the anchovy fillets, then carefully wrap up each parcel, making sure the paper folds are underneath and the carrot mixture on top.

4 Bake for 20 minutes and serve hot, in the paper, garnished with black olives and herb sprigs.

Chicken in a Tomato Coat

Chicken roasted with a coating of tomato sauce and fresh tomatoes.

INGREDIENTS

Serves 4–6

1.5–1.75kg/3–4^{1}/2lb free-range chicken

1 small onion

knob of butter

75ml/5 tbsp ready-made tomato sauce

30ml/2 tbsp chopped, mixed fresh herbs, such as parsley, tarragon, sage, basil and marjoram, or 10ml/2 tsp dried

small glass of dry white wine

2–3 small tomatoes, sliced

olive oil

little cornflour (optional)

salt and black pepper

1 Preheat the oven to 190°C/ 375°F/Gas 5. Place the chicken in a roasting tin. Place the onion, the knob of butter and some seasoning inside the chicken.

2 Spread most of the tomato sauce over the chicken and sprinkle with half the herbs and some seasoning. Pour the wine into the roasting tin.

3 Cover with foil, then roast for 1^{1}/2 hours, basting occasionally. Remove the foil, spread with the remaining sauce and the sliced tomatoes and drizzle with oil. Continue cooking for a further 20–30 minutes, or until the chicken is cooked through.

4 Sprinkle the remaining herbs over the chicken, then carve into portions. Thicken the sauce with a little cornflour if you wish.

Chicken Kiev

Cut through the crispy-coated chicken to reveal a creamy filling with just a hint of garlic.

INGREDIENTS

Serves 4

4 large chicken breasts, boned and
   skinned
15ml/1 tbsp lemon juice
115g/4oz/^{1}/$_2$ cup ricotta cheese
1 garlic clove, crushed
30ml/2 tbsp chopped fresh parsley
1.5ml/^{1}/$_4$ tsp freshly grated nutmeg
30ml/2 tbsp plain flour
pinch of cayenne pepper
1.5ml/^{1}/$_4$ tsp salt
115g/4oz/2 cups fresh white breadcrumbs
2 egg whites, lightly beaten
creamed potatoes, French beans and
   grilled tomatoes, to serve

1 Preheat the oven to 200°C/
400°F/Gas 6. Place the chicken breasts between two sheets of clear film and gently beat with a rolling pin until flattened. Sprinkle with the lemon juice.

2 Mix the ricotta cheese with the garlic, 15ml/1 tbsp of the chopped parsley and the nutmeg. Shape into four 5cm/2in long rolls.

3 Put one portion of the cheese and herb mixture in the centre of each chicken breast and fold the meat over, tucking in the edges to enclose the filling completely.

4 Secure the chicken with cock-tail sticks pushed through the centre of each. Mix together the flour, cayenne pepper and salt and use to dust the chicken.

5 Mix together the breadcrumbs and remaining parsley. Dip the chicken into the egg whites, then coat with the breadcrumbs. Chill for 30 minutes in the fridge, then dip into the egg white and bread-crumbs for a second time.

6 Put the chicken on a non-stick baking sheet. Bake in the pre-heated oven for 25 minutes or until the coating is golden brown and the chicken completely cooked. Remove the cocktail sticks and serve with creamed potatoes, French beans and grilled tomatoes.

Red-hot Chicken

A good party dish. The chicken is marinated the night before so all you have to do on the day is to cook it in a very hot oven and serve with wedges of lemon and a green salad.

INGREDIENTS

Serves 4

1.75kg/4–4^1/2lb chicken, cut into 8 pieces

juice of 1 large lemon

150ml/^{1}/4 pint/^{2}/3 cup natural low-fat
  yogurt

3 garlic cloves, crushed

30ml/2 tbsp olive oil

5ml/1 tsp ground turmeric

10ml/2 tsp paprika

5ml/1 tsp grated fresh root ginger or
  2.5ml/^{1}/2 tsp ground ginger

10ml/2 tsp garam masala

5ml/1 tsp salt

a few drops red food colouring (optional)

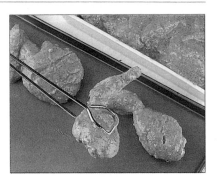

3 Mix together the remaining ingredients and pour the sauce over the chicken pieces, turning them to coat thoroughly. Cover with clear film and chill overnight.

4 Preheat the oven to 220°C/425°F/Gas 7. Remove the chicken from the marinade and arrange in a single layer on a shallow baking sheet. Bake for 15 minutes, turn over, and cook for a further 15 minutes or until tender.

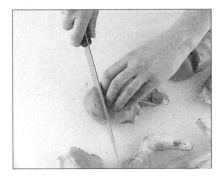

1 Skin the chicken pieces and cut two slits in each piece.

2 Arrange in a single layer in a glass or ceramic dish and pour over the lemon juice.

Chicken with Apricot and Pecan Baskets

The potato baskets make a pretty addition to the chicken and could easily have different fillings when you feel the need for a change.

INGREDIENTS

Serves 8

8 chicken breast fillets

25g/1oz/2 tbsp butter

6 mushrooms, chopped

15g/^{1}/2oz/1 tbsp chopped pecan nuts

115g/4oz/^{2}/3 cup chopped, cooked ham

50g/2oz/1 cup wholemeal breadcrumbs

15ml/1 tbsp chopped parsley, plus some
   whole leaves to garnish

salt and pepper

cocktail sticks to secure rolls

Sauce

15g/^{1}/2oz/1 tbsp cornflour

120ml/4fl oz/^{1}/2 cup white wine

50g/2oz/4 tbsp butter

50g/2oz/^{1}/4 cup apricot chutney

Potato baskets

4 large baking potatoes

175g/6oz sausagemeat

225g/8oz can apricots in natural juice,
   drained and quartered

1.5ml/^{1}/4 tsp cinnamon

2.5ml/^{1}/2 tsp grated orange rind

30ml/2 tbsp maple syrup

25g/1oz/2 tbsp butter

35g/1^1/4oz/^{1}/4 cup chopped pecan nuts,
   plus some pecan halves to garnish

1 Preheat the oven to 160°C/ 325°F/Gas 3. Put the chicken between two sheets of greaseproof paper and flatten with a meat mallet. Melt the butter in a pan and sauté the mushrooms, pecans and ham. Stir in the breadcrumbs, parsley and seasoning. Divide the mixture between the chicken breasts, roll up and secure each one with a cocktail stick. Chill.

2 Put the potatoes in the oven to bake. Mix the cornflour with a little of the wine to make a smooth paste. Put the remaining wine in a pan and add the paste. Cook, stirring, until smooth. Add the butter and apricot chutney and cook for 5 minutes, stirring constantly.

3 Place the chicken breasts in a shallow ovenproof dish and pour over the sauce. Bake in the oven (at the same temperature) for 20 minutes, basting several times.

4 When the potatoes are cooked, cut them in half and scoop out the inside, leaving a reasonable layer within the shell. Mash the potato and place in a mixing bowl.

5 Fry the sausagemeat and drain off any fat. Add the remaining ingredients and cook for 1 minute. Mix together the sausagemeat and potato and put in the potato shells. Sprinkle the pecan halves over the top, put in the oven with the chicken and bake for 30 minutes.

6 Remove the chicken and drain the sauce into a separate container. Slice the breasts, put on to plates and pour the sauce over the top. Serve with the potato baskets and garnish with parsley leaves.

Chicken Roule

A relatively simple dish to prepare, this recipe uses mince as a filling. It is rolled in chicken meat which is spread with a creamy garlic cheese that just melts in the mouth.

INGREDIENTS

Serves 4

4 boneless chicken breasts, about
    115g/4oz each
115g/4oz/1 cup minced beef
30ml/2 tbsp chopped fresh chives
225g/8oz Boursin or garlic
    cream cheese
30ml/2 tbsp clear honey
salt and black pepper

1 Preheat the oven to 190°C/
375°F/Gas 5. Place the chicken
breasts, side by side, between two
pieces of clear film. Beat with a
meat mallet until 1cm/¹/₂in thick
and joined together.

2 Place the minced beef in a large
pan. Fry for 3 minutes, add the
fresh chives and seasoning. Cool.

3 Place the chicken on a board
and spread with the cream
cheese.

4 Top with the mince mixture,
spreading it over evenly.

5 Roll up the chicken tightly to
form a sausage shape.

6 Brush with honey and place in
a roasting tin. Cook for 1 hour
in the preheated oven. Remove
from the tin and slice thinly. Serve
with freshly cooked vegetables.

Dijon Chicken Salad

An attractive dish to serve for lunch with herb and garlic bread.

INGREDIENTS

Serves 4

4 chicken breasts, boned and skinned

mixed salad leaves, e.g. frisée and oakleaf
   lettuce or radicchio, to serve

For the marinade

30ml/2 tbsp Dijon mustard

3 garlic cloves, crushed

15ml/1 tbsp grated onion

60ml/4 tbsp white wine

For the mustard dressing

30ml/2 tbsp tarragon wine vinegar

5ml/1 tsp Dijon mustard

5ml/1 tsp clear honey

90ml/6 tbsp olive oil

salt and black pepper

1 Mix all the marinade ingredients together in a shallow glass or earthenware dish that is large enough to hold the chicken in a single layer.

2 Turn the chicken over in the marinade to coat completely, cover with clear film and then chill in the fridge overnight.

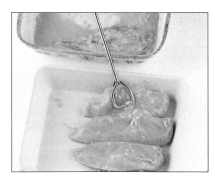

3 Preheat the oven to 190°C/375°F/Gas 5. Transfer the chicken and the marinade into an ovenproof dish, cover with foil and bake for about 35 minutes or until tender. Leave to cool.

4 Put all the mustard dressing ingredients into a screw-topped jar, shake vigorously to emulsify, and adjust the seasoning. (This can be made several days in advance and stored in the fridge.)

5 Slice the chicken thinly, fan out the slices and arrange on a serving dish with the salad leaves.

6 Spoon over some of the mustard dressing and serve.

Chicken and Fruit Salad

The chickens may be cooked a day before eating and the salad can be quickly put together for lunch.

Serves 8

4 sprigs tarragon or rosemary

2 x 1.75kg/4lb chickens

65g/2^1/2oz/5 tbsp softened butter

150ml/^{1}/4 pint/^{2}/3 cup chicken stock

150ml/^{1}/4 pint/^{2}/3 cup white wine

115g/4oz/1 cup walnut pieces

1 small cantaloupe melon

lettuce leaves

450g/1lb seedless grapes or stoned
   cherries

salt and black pepper

Dressing

30ml/2 tbsp tarragon vinegar

120ml/4 fl oz/^{1}/2 cup light olive oil

30ml/2 tbsp chopped mixed fresh herbs,
   e.g. parsley, mint and tarragon

1 Preheat the oven to 200°C/400°F/Gas 6. Put the herb sprigs inside the chickens and season. Tie the chickens with string. Spread the chickens with 50g/2oz/4 tbsp of the softened butter, place in a roasting tin and pour round the stock. Cover loosely with foil and roast for about 1^1/2 hours, basting twice, until browned and the juices run clear. Remove the chickens from the roasting tin.

2 Add the wine to the roasting tin. Bring to the boil and cook until syrupy. Strain and leave to cool. Heat the remaining butter in a frying pan and gently fry the walnuts until browned. Drain and cool. Scoop the melon into balls or into cubes, joint the chickens.

3 To make the dressing, whisk the vinegar and oil together with a little salt and freshly ground black pepper. Remove all the fat from the chicken juices and add these to the dressing with the herbs. Adjust the seasoning.

4 Arrange the chicken pieces on a bed of lettuce, scatter over the grapes or stoned cherries, melon balls or cubes and spoon over the herb dressing. Sprinkle with toasted walnuts.

ONE POT
DISHES &
CASSEROLES

~

Fragrant Chicken Curry with Thai Spices

This is a perfect curry for a party, as the chicken and sauce can be prepared in advance and combined at the last minute.

INGREDIENTS

Serves 4

45ml/3 tbsp oil

1 onion, roughly chopped

2 garlic cloves, crushed

15ml/1 tbsp Thai red curry paste

115g/4oz creamed coconut dissolved in
    900ml/1½ pints/3¾ cups
    boiling water

2 lemon grass stalks, roughly chopped

6 kaffir lime leaves, chopped

150ml/¼ pint/⅔ cup Greek-style yogurt

30ml/2 tbsp apricot jam

1 cooked chicken about 1.5kg/3–3½lb

30ml/2 tbsp chopped fresh coriander

salt and freshly ground black pepper

kaffir lime leaves, shredded coconut and
    fresh coriander, to garnish

boiled rice, to serve

1 Heat the oil in a heavy-based saucepan. Add the onion and garlic and sauté over a low heat for 5–10 minutes, until soft and translucent. Stir in the red curry paste and cook, stirring constantly, for 2–3 minutes.

2 Stir in the diluted creamed coconut, then add the lemon grass, lime leaves, yogurt and apricot jam. Stir thoroughly, cover and simmer over a low heat for 30 minutes.

3 Process the sauce in a blender or food processor, then strain it into a clean pan, pressing as much of the puréed mixture as possible through the strainer.

4 Remove the skin from the chicken, slice the meat off the bones and cut it into bite-size pieces. Add to the sauce.

5 Bring the sauce back to simmering point. If the sauce seems too thin, stir in a little additional creamed coconut to thicken and mix well. Stir in the fresh coriander and season to taste with salt and pepper. Transfer to a serving dish, garnish with extra lime leaves, shredded coconut and coriander and serve with rice.

Chicken with Onion Marmalade

An unusual whisky, honey and sesame seed paste enhances the flavour of chicken.

INGREDIENTS

Serves 4

25g/1oz/4 tbsp sesame seeds, crushed
2 garlic cloves, crushed
pinch of paprika
30ml/2 tbsp oil
30ml/2 tbsp whisky
30ml/2 tbsp clear honey
4 chicken portions
salt and freshly ground black pepper

For the marmalade

30ml/2 tbsp oil
2 large onions, finely sliced
1 green pepper, seeded and sliced
150ml/¼ pint/⅔ cup vegetable stock

1 Preheat the oven to 190°C/ 375°F/Gas 5. Mix together the sesame seeds, garlic, paprika, oil, whisky and honey to make a paste. Season to taste. Add a little water if the paste is too thick.

2 Slash the chicken portions and arrange them in an ovenproof dish. Spread the paste over the chicken. Roast for 40 minutes, or until cooked through and tender.

3 Meanwhile, make the onion marmalade. Heat the oil in a frying pan and fry the onion slices over a medium-high heat for 15 minutes. Add the green pepper and fry for a further 5 minutes. Stir in the stock, season with salt and pepper and cook gently, stirring occasionally, for about 20 minutes. Serve warm with the cooked chicken.

VARIATION

Instead of making cuts in the chicken portions, ease the skin away from the flesh and push the paste underneath. This keeps the flesh wonderfully moist.

Chicken with Wild Mushrooms

Tender chicken slices are folded into a rich soured cream sauce spiked with brandy and vermouth.

INGREDIENTS

Serves 4

30ml/2 tbsp oil
1 leek, finely chopped
4 chicken breasts, sliced
225g/8oz/2 cups wild mushrooms, sliced if large
15ml/1 tbsp brandy
pinch of grated nutmeg
1.5ml/¼ tsp chopped fresh thyme
150ml/¼ pint/⅔ cup dry white vermouth
150ml/¼ pint/⅔ cup chicken stock
6 green olives, stoned and quartered
150ml/¼ pint/⅔ cup soured cream
salt and freshly ground black pepper
thyme sprigs and croûtons, to garnish

1 Heat the oil in a frying pan. Add the chopped leek and fry, stirring occasionally, until softened, but not browned. Add the slices of chicken and the mushrooms. Fry over a medium heat, stirring occasionally, until the chicken is just beginning to brown.

2 Pour over the brandy and ignite carefully with a match. When the flames have died down, stir in the nutmeg, thyme, vermouth and stock and season with salt and pepper.

3 Bring to the boil, then simmer for 5 minutes. Stir in the olives and most of the soured cream and reheat gently. Garnish with the remaining soured cream, the thyme sprigs and croûtons.

Chicken with Sage, Prunes and Brandy

This stir-fry has a very rich sauce based on a good brandy – use the best you can afford.

INGREDIENTS

Serves 4

115g/4oz prunes

1.5kg/3–3^{1}/2lb boneless chicken breast

300ml/^{1}/2 pint/1^{1}/4 cups cognac or brandy

15ml/1 tbsp fresh sage, chopped

150g/5oz smoked bacon, in one piece

50g/2oz/4 tbsp butter

24 baby onions, peeled and quartered

salt and black pepper

fresh sage sprigs, to garnish

1 Stone the prunes and cut them into slivers. Remove the skin from the chicken and cut the breast into thin pieces.

2 Mix together the prunes, chicken, cognac and chopped sage in a non-metallic dish. Cover and leave to marinate overnight.

3 Next day, strain the chicken and prunes, reserving the cognac marinade mixture, and pat dry on kitchen towels.

4 Cut the smoked bacon into dice and set aside.

5 Heat the wok and add half the butter. When melted, add the onions and stir-fry for 4 minutes until crisp and golden. Set aside.

6 Add the bacon to the wok and stir-fry for 1 minute until it begins to release some fat. Add the remaining butter and stir-fry the chicken and prunes for 3–4 minutes until crisp and golden. Push the chicken mixture to one side in the wok, add the cognac and simmer until thickened. Stir the chicken into the sauce, season well with salt and pepper, and serve garnished with sage.

Coq au Vin

This classic combination, served in a rich, thick sauce, is very easy to prepare and requires only a little last-minute attention, so it is an ideal dish for entertaining.

INGREDIENTS

Serves 4

1 small chicken, about 1.3kg/3lb, or 4 chicken pieces
seasoned plain flour, for coating
30ml/2 tbsp sunflower oil
25g/1oz/2 tbsp butter
115g/4oz unsmoked streaky bacon, finely chopped
2 garlic cloves
450ml/¾ pint/1¾ cups red wine
1 bay leaf
2 thyme sprigs
250g/9oz shallots, peeled
115g/4oz button mushrooms, halved if large
10ml/2 tsp plain flour
salt and freshly ground black pepper

1 Preheat the oven to 180°C/ 350°F/Gas 4. Remove and discard any skin and fat from the chicken and, using poultry shears or a sharp knife, cut the chicken into four or eight pieces. Place a little seasoned flour in a large plastic bag, add the chicken pieces and shake to coat evenly.

2 Heat half the oil and half the butter in a large flameproof casserole. Add the bacon and garlic and fry, stirring frequently, for 3–4 minutes. Add the chicken pieces and fry over a medium heat until lightly browned all over. Add the wine, bay leaf and thyme and bring to the boil. Cover, transfer to the oven and cook for 1 hour.

3 Cook the shallots in boiling salted water for 10 minutes. Heat the remaining oil in a frying pan and fry the shallots for 3–4 minutes, until beginning to brown. Add the mushrooms and fry for a further 2–3 minutes.

4 Stir the shallots and mushrooms into the casserole with the chicken and cook for a further 8–10 minutes. Using a fork, blend the flour with the remaining butter to make a thick paste.

5 Transfer the chicken pieces, shallots and mushrooms to a serving dish and keep warm. Bring the cooking liquid to the boil and add small pieces of the flour paste, stirring vigorously after each addition. When all the paste has been added and the sauce is thick, pour it over the chicken pieces and serve immediately.

Chicken Paella

There are many variations of this basic recipe. Any seasonal vegetables can be added, together with mussels and other shellfish. Serve straight from the pan.

INGREDIENTS

Serves 4

4 chicken legs (thighs and drumsticks)

60ml/4 tbsp olive oil

1 large onion, finely chopped

1 garlic clove, crushed

5ml/1 tsp ground turmeric

115g/4oz chorizo sausage or smoked ham

225g/8oz/generous 1 cup long grain rice

600ml/1 pint/$2^1/2$ cups chicken stock

4 tomatoes, skinned, seeded and chopped

1 red pepper, seeded and sliced

115g/4oz/1 cup frozen peas

salt and black pepper

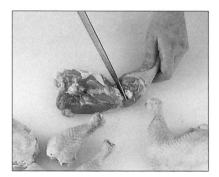

1 Preheat the oven to 180°C/ 350°F/Gas 4. Cut the chicken legs in half.

2 Heat the oil in a 30cm/12in paella pan or large flameproof casserole and brown the chicken pieces on both sides. Add the onion and garlic and stir in the turmeric. Cook for 2 minutes.

3 Slice the sausage or dice the ham and add to the pan, with the rice and stock. Bring to the boil and season to taste, cover and bake for 15 minutes.

4 Remove from the oven and add the chopped tomatoes and sliced red pepper and frozen peas. Return to the oven and cook for a further 10–15 minutes or until the chicken is tender and the rice has absorbed the stock.

Risotto

An Italian dish made with short grain arborio rice which gives a creamy consistency to this easy one-pan recipe.

INGREDIENTS

Serves 4

15ml/1 tbsp oil

175g/6oz/1 cup Arborio rice

1 onion, chopped

225g/8oz/2 cups minced chicken

600ml/1 pint/2$^{1}/_{2}$ cups chicken stock

1 red pepper, seeded and chopped

1 yellow pepper, seeded and chopped

75g/3oz/$^{3}/_{4}$ cup frozen green beans

115g/4oz/1$^{1}/_{2}$ cups chestnut mushrooms, sliced

15ml/1 tbsp chopped fresh parsley

salt and black pepper

fresh parsley, to garnish

3 Pour in the stock and bring to the boil.

4 Stir in the peppers and reduce the heat. Cook for 10 minutes.

5 Add the green beans and mushrooms and cook for a further 10 minutes.

6 Stir in the fresh parsley and season well to taste. Cook for 10 minutes or until the liquid has been absorbed. Serve garnished with fresh parsley.

1 Heat the oil in a large frying pan. Add the rice and cook for 2 minutes until transparent.

2 Add the onion and minced chicken. Cook for 5 minutes, stirring occasionally.

French-style Pot-roast Poussins

An incredibly simple dish to make that looks and tastes extra special.

INGREDIENTS

Serves 4

15ml/1 tbsp olive oil

1 onion, sliced

1 large garlic clove, sliced

50g/2oz/scant¹/₂ cup diced lightly smoked
  bacon

2 fresh poussins (just under 450g/1lb each)

30ml/2 tbsp melted butter

2 baby celery hearts, each cut into 4

8 baby carrots

2 small courgettes, cut into chunks

8 small new potatoes

600ml/1 pint/2¹/₂ cups chicken stock

150ml/¹/₄ pint/²/₃ cup dry white wine

1 bay leaf

2 fresh thyme sprigs

2 fresh rosemary sprigs

15g/¹/₂oz/1 tbsp butter, softened

15ml/1 tbsp plain flour

salt and black pepper

fresh herbs, to garnish

1 Preheat the oven to 190°C/
375°F/Gas 5. Heat the olive oil
in a large flameproof casserole and
add the onion, garlic and bacon.
Sauté for 5–6 minutes, until the
onions have softened.

2 Brush the poussins with a little
of the melted butter and season
well. Lay on top of the onion
mixture and arrange the prepared
vegetables around them. Add the
chicken stock, wine and herbs.

3 Cover, bake for 20 minutes,
then remove the lid and brush
the birds with the remaining
melted butter. Bake for a further
25–30 minutes until golden.

4 Transfer the poussins to a
warmed serving platter and
cut each in half with poultry shears
or scissors. Remove the vegetables
with a draining spoon and arrange
them round the birds. Cover with
foil and keep warm.

5 Discard the herbs from the pan
juices. In a bowl mix together
the butter and flour to form a
paste. Bring the liquid in the pan
to the boil and then whisk in
teaspoonfuls of the paste until
thickened. Season the sauce and
serve with the poussins and
vegetables, garnished with
fresh herbs.

Chicken with Asparagus

Canned asparagus may be used instead of fresh, but will not require any cooking – simply add at the very end to warm through.

Serves 4

4 large chicken breasts, boned and
   skinned
15ml/1 tbsp ground coriander
30ml/2 tbsp olive oil
20 slender asparagus spears, cut
   into 7.5–10cm/3–4 in lengths
300ml/$^1/_2$ pint/1$^1/_4$ cups chicken stock
15ml/1 tbsp cornflour
15ml/1 tbsp lemon juice
salt and black pepper
15ml/1 tbsp chopped fresh parsley

1 Divide the chicken breasts into two natural fillets. Place each between two sheets of clear film and flatten to a thickness of 5mm/$^1/_4$ in with a rolling pin. Cut into 2.5cm/1in strips diagonally. Sprinkle over the coriander and toss to coat each piece.

2 Heat the oil in a large frying pan and fry the chicken very quickly in small batches for 3–4 minutes until lightly coloured. Season each batch with a little salt and freshly ground black pepper. Remove and keep warm while frying the rest of the chicken.

3 Add the asparagus and chicken stock to the pan and bring to the boil. Cook for a further 4–5 minutes, or until tender.

4 Mix the cornflour to a paste with a little cold water and stir into the sauce to thicken. Return the chicken to the pan and add the lemon juice. Reheat and then serve immediately, garnished with fresh parsley.

Chicken Sauce Piquante

Sauce Piquante goes with everything that runs, flies or swims in Louisiana – you will even find Alligator Sauce Piquante on menus. It is based on the brown Cajun roux and chilli peppers give it heat: vary the heat by the number you use.

Serves 4

4 chicken legs or 2 legs and 2 breasts

75ml/3fl oz/^{1}/$_3$ cup cooking oil

50g/2oz/^{1}/$_2$ cup plain flour

1 medium onion, chopped

2 celery sticks, sliced

1 green pepper, seeded and diced

2 garlic cloves, crushed

1 bay leaf

2.5ml/^{1}/$_2$ tsp dried thyme

2.5ml/^{1}/$_2$ tsp dried oregano

1–2 red chilli peppers, seeded and finely
    chopped

400g/14oz can tomatoes, chopped, with
    the juice

300ml/^{1}/$_2$ pint/1^1/$_4$ cups chicken stock

salt and black pepper

watercress to garnish

boiled potatoes to serve

1 Halve the chicken legs through the joint, or the breasts across the middle, to give 8 pieces.

2 In a heavy frying pan, fry the chicken pieces in the oil until brown on all sides, setting them aside as they are done.

3 Strain the oil from the pan into a heavy flameproof casserole. Heat it and stir in the flour. Stir constantly over a low heat until the roux is the colour of peanut butter.

4 Immediately the roux reaches the right stage, tip in the onion, celery and pepper and stir over the heat for 2–3 minutes.

5 Add the garlic, bay leaf, thyme, oregano and chilli pepper(s). Stir for 1 minute, then turn down

the heat and stir in the tomatoes with their juice.

6 Return the casserole to the heat and gradually stir in the stock. Add the chicken pieces, cover and leave to simmer for 45 minutes, until the chicken is tender.

7 If there is too much sauce or if it looks too runny, remove the lid for the last 10–15 minutes of the cooking time and turn up the heat a little.

8 Check the seasoning and serve garnished with watercress and accompanied by boiled potatoes.

COOK'S TIP

If you prefer to err on the side of caution with chilli heat, use just 1 chilli pepper and hot up the seasoning at the end with a dash or two of Tabasco sauce.
The oil in chilli peppers clings to your skin and could hurt if you then rub your eyes. Scrape out the seeds under running cold water and wash your hands after handling chillies.

Chicken with Chianti

Together the robust, full-flavoured red wine and red pesto give this sauce a rich colour and almost spicy flavour, while the grapes add a delicious sweetness.

Serves 4

45ml/3 tbsp olive oil

4 part-boned skinless chicken breasts

1 medium red onion

30ml/2 tbsp red pesto

300ml/½ pint/1¼ cups Chianti

300ml/½ pint/1¼ cups water

115g/4oz red grapes, halved lengthways
    and seeded, if necessary

salt and freshly ground black pepper

fresh basil leaves, to garnish

rocket salad, to serve

1 Heat 30ml/2 tbsp of the oil in a large pan, add the chicken and sauté over a medium heat for 5 minutes, until golden. Remove and drain on kitchen paper.

2 Halve the onion through the root. Trim off the root, then slice the onion halves lengthways.

3 Heat the remaining oil in the pan and add the onion wedges and red pesto. Cook gently, stirring constantly, for about 3 minutes, or until the onion has softened but not browned.

4 Add the Chianti and water to the pan and bring to the boil, stirring constantly. Then return the chicken to the pan and season with salt and pepper to taste.

5 Reduce the heat, then cover the pan and simmer gently, stirring occasionally, for about 20 minutes, or until the chicken is tender and cooked through.

6 Add the grapes to the pan and cook over a low to medium heat until the grapes are just heated through. Taste the sauce and adjust the seasoning, if necessary. Transfer the chicken to a warm serving dish and spoon over the sauce. Garnish with fresh basil and serve immediately, accompanied by the rocket salad.

Chicken with Tomatoes and Prawns

This Piedmontese dish was created especially for Napoleon after the battle of Marengo. Versions of it appear in both Italian and French recipe books.

INGREDIENTS

Serves 4

120ml/4fl oz/½ cup olive oil
8 skinless chicken thighs
1 onion, finely chopped
1 celery stick, finely chopped
1 garlic clove, crushed
350g/12oz ripe Italian plum tomatoes,
    peeled and roughly chopped
250ml/8fl oz/1 cup dry white wine
2.5ml/½ tsp chopped fresh rosemary
15g/½oz/1 tbsp butter
8 small triangles of thinly sliced white
    bread, without crusts
175g/6oz large raw prawns, peeled
salt and freshly ground black pepper
finely chopped flat leaf parsley, to garnish

1 Heat 30ml/2 tbsp of the oil in a frying pan and sauté the chicken over a medium heat for about 5 minutes, until light brown. Transfer to a flameproof casserole.

VARIATION

❧

To make the dish look more like its original, authentic version, garnish it with a few large crayfish or prawns in their shells.

2 Add the onion and celery to the frying pan and sauté, stirring frequently, for 3 minutes, until softened. Add the garlic, tomatoes, wine, rosemary and salt and pepper. Bring to the boil, stirring.

3 Pour the tomato sauce over the chicken. Cover and cook gently for 40 minutes, or until cooked.

4 Heat the remaining oil and the butter in a frying pan. Fry the bread triangles until crisp and golden on both sides. Drain on kitchen paper.

5 Add the prawns to the casserole and heat through. Dip a corner of the bread triangles in parsley, garnish the chicken and serve.

Chicken with Lemon and Herbs

The herbs can be changed according to what is available; for example, parsley or thyme could be used instead of tarragon and fennel.

INGREDIENTS

Serves 2

50g/2oz/4 tbsp butter

2 spring onions, white part only, finely chopped

15ml/1 tbsp chopped fresh tarragon

15ml/1 tbsp chopped fresh fennel

juice of 1 lemon

4 chicken thighs

salt and black pepper

lemon slices and herb sprigs, to garnish

1 Preheat the grill to moderate. In a small saucepan, melt the butter, then add the spring onions, herbs, lemon juice and seasoning.

2 Brush the chicken generously with the herb mixture, then grill for 10–12 minutes, basting frequently with the herb mixture.

3 Turn over, baste again, then cook for a further 10 minutes or until the juices run clear.

4 Serve garnished with lemon and herbs and with any remaining herb mixture.

Chicken with Red Cabbage

Chestnuts and red cabbage make a colourful winter dish.

INGREDIENTS

Serves 4

50g/2oz/4 tbsp butter

4 large chicken portions, halved

1 onion, chopped

500g/1¼lb red cabbage, finely shredded

4 juniper berries, crushed

12 cooked peeled chestnuts

120ml/4fl oz/½ cup full-bodied red wine

salt and black pepper

1 Heat the butter in a heavy flameproof casserole and lightly brown the chicken pieces. Transfer to a plate.

2 Add the onion to the casserole and fry gently until soft and light golden brown. Stir the cabbage and juniper berries into the casserole, season and cook over a moderate heat for 6–7 minutes, stirring once or twice.

3 Stir the chestnuts into the casserole, then tuck the chicken pieces under the cabbage so they are on the bottom of the casserole. Pour in the red wine.

4 Cover and cook gently for about 40 minutes until the chicken juices run clear and the cabbage is very tender. Check the seasoning and serve.

Chicken in Creamy Orange Sauce

This sauce is deceptively creamy – in fact it is made with low-fat fromage frais, which is virtually fat-free. The brandy adds a richer flavour, but is optional – omit it if you prefer and use orange juice alone.

INGREDIENTS

Serves 4

8 chicken thighs or drumsticks, skinned

45ml/3 tbsp brandy

300ml/$^1/_2$ pint/1$^1/_4$ cups orange juice

3 spring onions, chopped

10ml/2 tsp cornflour

90ml/3fl oz/$^1/_3$ cup low-fat fromage frais

salt and black pepper

rice or pasta and green salad, to serve

1 Fry the chicken pieces without fat in a non-stick or heavy pan, turning until evenly browned.

2 Stir in the brandy, orange juice and spring onions. Bring to the boil, then cover and simmer for 15 minutes, or until the chicken is tender and the juices run clear, not pink, when pierced.

3 Blend the cornflour with a little water then mix into the fromage frais. Stir this into the sauce and stir over a moderate heat until boiling.

4 Adjust the seasoning and serve with boiled rice or pasta and green salad.

COOK'S TIP

Cornflour helps to stabilize the fromage frais and stop it from curdling.

Tuscan Chicken

This simple peasant casserole has all the flavours of traditional Tuscan ingredients. The wine can be replaced by chicken stock.

INGREDIENTS

Serves 4

8 chicken thighs, skinned

5ml/1 tsp olive oil

1 medium onion, thinly sliced

2 red peppers, seeded and sliced

1 garlic clove, crushed

300ml/^{1}/$_2$ pint/1^1/$_4$ cups passata

150ml/^{1}/$_4$ pint/^{2}/$_3$ cup dry white wine

large sprig fresh oregano, or 5ml/1 tsp
   dried oregano

400g/14oz can cannellini beans, drained

45ml/3 tbsp fresh breadcrumbs

salt and black pepper

1 Fry the chicken in the oil in a non-stick or heavy pan until golden brown. Remove and keep hot. Add the onion and peppers to the pan and gently sauté until softened, but not brown. Stir in the garlic.

2 Add the chicken, passata, wine and oregano. Season well, bring to the boil then cover the pan tightly.

3 Lower the heat and simmer gently, stirring occasionally for 30–35 minutes or until the chicken is tender and the juices run clear, not pink, when pierced with the point of a knife.

4 Stir in the cannellini beans and simmer for a further 5 minutes until heated through. Sprinkle with the breadcrumbs and cook under a hot grill until golden brown.

Chicken with Blackberries and Lemon

This delicious stew combines some wonderful flavours. The red wine and blackberries give it a dramatic appearance.

INGREDIENTS

Serves 4

4 part-boned chicken breasts
25g/1oz/2 tbsp butter
15ml/1 tbsp sunflower oil
25g/1oz/4 tbsp flour
150ml/^{1}/4 pint/^{2}/3 cup red wine
150ml/^{1}/4 pint/^{2}/3 cup chicken stock
grated rind of ^{1}/2 orange plus 15ml/1 tbsp juice
3 sprigs lemon balm, finely chopped, plus 1 sprig to garnish
150ml/^{1}/4 pint/^{2}/3 cup double cream
1 egg yolk
115g/4oz/1 cup fresh blackberries, plus 50g/2oz/^{1}/2 cup to garnish
salt and black pepper

1 Preheat the oven to 180°C/ 350°F/Gas 4. Remove any skin from the chicken, and season the meat. Heat the butter and oil in a frying pan, fry the chicken to seal it, then transfer to a casserole dish. Stir the flour into the pan, then add the wine and stock and bring to the boil. Add the orange rind and juice, and the chopped lemon balm. Pour over the chicken.

2 Cover the casserole and cook in the oven for about 40 minutes.

3 Blend the cream with the egg yolk, add some of the liquid from the casserole and stir back into the dish with the blackberries (reserving those for the garnish). Cover and cook for another 10–15 minutes. Serve garnished with the rest of the blackberries and the sprig of lemon balm.

Hunter's Chicken

This traditional dish sometimes has strips of green pepper in the sauce for extra colour and flavour instead of the fresh mushrooms.

INGREDIENTS

Serves 4

15g/½oz/1 cup dried porcini
    mushrooms

250ml/8fl oz/1 cup warm water

30ml/2 tbsp olive oil

15g/½oz/1 tbsp butter

4 skinless chicken pieces

1 large onion, thinly sliced

400g/14oz can chopped tomatoes

150ml/¼ pint/⅔ cup red wine

1 garlic clove, crushed

leaves of 1 sprig fresh rosemary,
    finely chopped

115g/4oz/1¼ cups fresh field mushrooms,
    thinly sliced

salt and freshly ground black pepper

fresh rosemary sprigs, to garnish

creamed potatoes or polenta,
    to serve (optional)

1 Put the porcini in a small bowl, add the warm water and set aside to soak for 20–30 minutes. Remove from the liquid and squeeze the porcini over the bowl. Strain the liquid and reserve. Finely chop the porcini.

2 Heat the oil and butter in a large flameproof casserole until foaming. Add the chicken and sauté over a medium heat for 5 minutes, or until golden. Remove and drain on kitchen paper.

3 Add the onion and porcini to the pan. Cook gently, stirring frequently, for about 3 minutes, or until the onion has softened. Stir in the chopped tomatoes, wine and reserved mushroom soaking liquid, then add the crushed garlic and chopped rosemary and season with salt and pepper to taste. Bring to the boil, stirring constantly.

4 Return the chicken to the pan and coat with the sauce. Cover and simmer gently for 30 minutes.

5 Stir in the fresh mushrooms. Continue simmering gently for 10 minutes, or until the chicken is tender. Serve hot, with creamed potato or polenta, if you like, and garnished with rosemary.

Jambalaya

Cajun cooking, a culinary style developed by French peasant settlers in Louisiana, is distinguished by its use of fiery spices.

INGREDIENTS

Serves 4

30ml/2 tbsp oil

225g/8oz boneless skinless chicken, cubed

225g/8oz chorizo sausage,
    cut into chunks

3 celery sticks, chopped

1 red pepper, seeded and chopped

1 green pepper, seeded and chopped

250g/9oz/generous 1 cup long grain rice

200g/7oz can chopped tomatoes

600ml/1 pint/2½ cups chicken stock

celery leaves, to garnish

For the Cajun spice mix

5ml/1 tsp black peppercorns

5ml/1 tsp cumin seeds

5ml/1 tsp white mustard seeds

10ml/2 tsp paprika

5ml/1 tsp chilli powder

5ml/1 tsp dried oregano

10ml/2 tsp dried thyme

5ml/1 tsp salt

2 garlic cloves, finely chopped

1 onion, sliced

1 To make the Cajun spice mix, dry-fry the peppercorns, cumin and mustard seeds over a medium heat until they give off their aroma. Grind the dry-fried spices, then add the paprika, chilli powder, oregano, thyme and salt and grind again. Put the spice mixture into a food processor with the garlic and onion and process until combined.

2 Heat the oil in a heavy-based frying pan. Fry the chicken and chorizo sausage until lightly browned. Remove from the pan and set aside. Fry the celery and peppers for 2–3 minutes. Return the chicken and sausage to the pan.

3 Add the spice mix and cook, stirring, for 2–3 minutes. Add the rice, the tomatoes and stock and bring to the boil, stirring constantly. Lower the heat, cover the pan and simmer gently for 15–20 minutes, until the rice is tender and all the liquid has been absorbed. Garnish with celery leaves and serve immediately.

COOK'S TIP

For a milder dish, use less chilli powder in the spice mix.

Chicken Cordon Bleu

A rich dish, popular with cheese lovers. Serve simply with green beans and tiny baked potatoes, cut and filled with cream cheese.

INGREDIENTS

Serves 4

4 chicken breasts, boned and
    skinned
4 slices cooked lean ham
60ml/4 tbsp grated Gruyère or
    Emmental cheese
30ml/2 tbsp olive oil
115g/4oz button mushrooms, sliced
60ml/4 tbsp white wine
salt and black pepper
watercress, to garnish

1 Place the chicken between two pieces of clear film and flatten to a thickness of 5mm/¼in with a rolling pin. Place the chicken breasts, outer side down, on the board and lay a slice of ham on each. Divide the cheese between the chicken and season with a little salt and freshly ground pepper.

2 Fold the chicken breasts in half and secure with wooden cocktail sticks, making a large "stitch" to hold the pieces together.

3 Heat the oil in a large frying pan and brown the chicken parcels on all sides. Remove to a dish and keep warm.

4 Add the mushrooms to the pan and cook for several minutes to brown lightly. Replace the chicken and pour over the wine, cover, and cook gently for 15–20 minutes until tender. Remove the cocktail sticks and arrange on a serving dish with a bunch of watercress.

Chicken with Sloe Gin and Juniper

Juniper is used in the manufacture of gin, and the reinforcement of the flavour by using both sloe gin and juniper is delicious. Sloe gin is easy to make, but can also be bought ready-made.

INGREDIENTS

Serves 8

25g/1oz/2 tbsp butter

30ml/2 tbsp sunflower oil

8 chicken breast fillets

350g/12oz carrots, cooked

1 clove garlic, crushed

15ml/1 tbsp finely chopped parsley

50ml/2fl oz/¼ cup chicken stock

50ml/2fl oz/¼ cup red wine

50ml/2fl oz/¼ cup sloe gin

5ml/1 tsp crushed juniper berries

salt and black pepper

chopped fresh basil, to garnish

1 Melt the butter with the oil in a frying pan, and fry the chicken until browned on all sides.

2 In a food processor or blender, combine all the remaining ingredients except the basil, and blend to a smooth purée. If the mixture seems too thick add a little more red wine or water.

3 Put the chicken breast in a clean pan, pour the sauce over the top and cook over a medium heat until the chicken is cooked through – about 15 minutes. Adjust the seasoning and serve garnished with chopped fresh basil.

Chicken with Figs and Mint

Refreshing mint and orange flavours go well with chicken.

INGREDIENTS

Serves 4

500g/1¹/4lb/3¹/3 cups dried figs
¹/2 bottle sweet, fruity white wine
4 boneless chicken breasts, about
    175–225g/6–8oz each
15ml/1 tbsp butter
30ml/2 tbsp dark orange marmalade
10 mint leaves, finely chopped, plus a few
    more to garnish
juice of ¹/2 lemon
salt and black pepper

1 Place the figs in a pan with the wine and bring to the boil, then simmer very gently for about 1 hour. Leave to cool and refrigerate overnight.

2 Fry the chicken breasts in the butter until they are cooked. Remove and keep warm. Drain any fat from the pan and pour in the juice from the figs. Boil and reduce to about 150ml/¹/4 pint/²/3 cup.

3 Add the marmalade, chopped mint leaves and lemon juice, and simmer for a few minutes. Season to taste. When the sauce is thick and shiny, pour it over the meat, garnish with the figs and mint leaves and serve.

GRILLS &
BARBECUES

Citrus Kebabs

Serve on a bed of lettuce leaves and garnish with fresh mint and orange and lemon slices.

INGREDIENTS

Serves 4

4 chicken breasts, skinned and boned
sprigs fresh mint, to garnish
orange, lemon or lime slices, to garnish
   (optional)

For the marinade
finely grated rind and juice of $^1/_2$ orange
finely grated rind and juice of $^1/_2$ small
   lemon or lime
30ml/2 tbsp olive oil
30ml/2 tbsp clear honey
30ml/2 tbsp chopped fresh mint
1.5ml/$^1/_4$ tsp ground cumin
salt and black pepper

1 Cut the chicken into cubes of approximately 2.5cm/1in.

2 Mix the marinade ingredients together in a glass or ceramic bowl, add the chicken cubes and leave to marinate for at least 2 hours.

3 Thread the chicken pieces on to skewers and grill or barbecue over low coals for 15 minutes, basting with the marinade and turning frequently. Serve garnished with extra mint and citrus slices if desired.

Minty Yogurt Chicken

Chicken marinated with yogurt, mint, lemon and honey and grilled.

INGREDIENTS

Serves 4

8 chicken thigh portions, skinned
15ml/1 tbsp clear honey
30ml/2 tbsp lime or lemon juice
30ml/2 tbsp natural yogurt
60ml/4 tbsp chopped fresh mint
salt and black pepper
new potatoes and a tomato salad,
   to serve

1 Slash the chicken flesh at regular intervals with a sharp knife. Place in a bowl.

2 Mix together the honey, lime or lemon juice, yogurt, seasoning and half the mint.

3 Spoon the marinade over the chicken and leave to marinate for 30 minutes. Line the grill pan with foil and cook the chicken under a moderately hot grill until thoroughly cooked and golden brown, turning the chicken occasionally during cooking.

4 Sprinkle with the remaining mint and serve with the potatoes and tomato salad.

Grilled Spatchcocked Poussins

Grilled poussins with an onion and herb dressing.

INGREDIENTS

Serves 4

4 poussins, about 450g/1lb each,
    spatchcocked
olive oil
salt and black pepper

For the onion and herb sauce
30ml/2 tbsp dry sherry
30ml/2 tbsp lemon juice
30ml/2 tbsp olive oil
50g/2oz spring onions, chopped
1 garlic clove, finely chopped
60ml/4 tbsp chopped mixed fresh herbs
    such as tarragon, parsley, thyme,
    marjoram, lemon balm

1 Preheat the grill to high, or prepare a charcoal barbecue.

2 Season the spatchcocked birds, then brush them with a little olive oil. Set them on the rack in the grill pan, about 10cm/4in from the heat, or on the barbecue 15cm/6in above the coals.

3 Cook for 20–25 minutes or until tender. Turn and brush with more oil halfway through the cooking time.

4 Meanwhile, to make the sauce, whisk together the sherry, lemon juice, olive oil, spring onions and garlic. Season with salt and pepper.

5 When the poussins are done, transfer them to a deep serving platter. Whisk the herbs into the sauce, then spoon it over the birds. Cover tightly with another platter or with foil and leave to rest for 15 minutes before serving.

Grilled Chicken Salad with Lavender

Lavender may seem like an odd salad ingredient, but its delightful scent has a natural affinity with sweet garlic, orange and other wild herbs. A serving of polenta makes this salad both filling and delicious.

INGREDIENTS

Serves 4

4 chicken breasts, boned

900ml/1 1/2 pints/3 3/4 cups light chicken stock

175g/6oz/1 cup fine polenta

50g/2oz/4tbsp butter

450g/1lb young spinach

175g/6oz lamb's lettuce

8 sprigs fresh lavender

8 small tomatoes, halved

salt and black pepper

Lavender Marinade

6 fresh lavender flowers

10ml/2 tsp finely grated orange rind

2 cloves garlic, crushed

10ml/2 tsp clear honey

salt

30ml/2 tbsp olive oil

10ml/2 tsp chopped fresh thyme

10ml/2 tsp chopped fresh marjoram

1 To make the marinade, strip the lavender flowers from the stems and combine with the orange rind, garlic, honey and salt. Add the olive oil and herbs. Slash the chicken deeply, spread the mixture over the chicken and leave to marinate in a cool place for at least 20 minutes.

2 To cook the polenta, bring the chicken stock to the boil in a heavy saucepan. Add the polenta in a steady stream, stirring all the time until thick: this will take 2–3 minutes. Turn the cooked polenta out on to a 2.5cm/1in deep buttered tray and allow to cool.

3 Heat the grill to a moderate temperature. (If using a barbecue, let the embers settle to a steady glow.) Grill the chicken for about 15 minutes, turning once.

4 Cut the polenta into 2.5cm/1in cubes with a wet knife. Heat the butter in a large frying pan and fry the polenta until golden.

5 Wash the salad leaves and spin dry, then divide among 4 large plates. Slice each chicken breast and lay over the salad. Place the polenta among the salad, decorate with sprigs of lavender and tomatoes, season and serve.

Blackened Cajun Chicken and Corn

This is a classic Cajun method of grilling or barbecuing poultry in a spiced coating.

INGREDIENTS

Serves 4

8 chicken joints (drumsticks or thighs)

2 corn cobs

10ml/2 tsp garlic salt

10ml/2 tsp freshly ground black pepper

7.5ml/1½ tsp ground cumin

7.5ml/1½ tsp paprika

5ml/1 tsp cayenne pepper

45ml/3 tbsp melted butter

chopped parsley, to garnish

1 Trim any excess fat from the chicken, but leave the skin in place. Slash the thickest parts with a knife to allow the flavours of the coating to penetrate the meat.

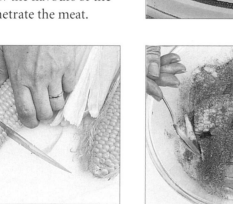

2 Pull the husks and silks off the corn cobs, then thoroughly rinse them under cold running water and pat them dry with kitchen paper. Cut the cobs into slices about 4–5cm/1½–2in thick, using a heavy kitchen knife.

3 In a small bowl, mix together the garlic salt, black pepper, cumin, paprika and cayenne pepper. Brush the chicken and corn with the melted butter and sprinkle the spices over them. Toss well to coat evenly.

4 Cook the chicken pieces under a preheated grill or on a barbecue for about 25 minutes, turning occasionally. Add the corn after 15 minutes, and grill, turning often, until golden brown. Serve garnished with chopped parsley.

Lemon Chicken with Guacamole Sauce

*The avocado sauce makes an
unusual accompaniment to the
grilled chicken.*

INGREDIENTS

Serves 4

juice of 2 lemons

45ml/3 tbsp olive oil

2 garlic cloves, crushed

4 chicken breast halves, about 200g/7oz
   each

2 beefsteak tomatoes, cored and cut in half

salt and black pepper

chopped fresh coriander, for garnishing

For the sauce

1 ripe avocado

50ml/2 fl oz/¼ cup sour cream

45ml/3 tbsp fresh lemon juice

25ml/½ tsp salt

50ml/2 fl oz/¼ cup water

1 Combine the lemon juice, oil,
garlic, ½ tsp salt, and a little
pepper in a bowl. Stir to mix.

2 Arrange the chicken breasts, in
one layer, in a shallow glass or
ceramic dish. Pour over the lemon
mixture and turn to coat evenly.
Cover and let stand at least 1 hour
at room temperature, or refrigerate
overnight.

3 For the sauce, cut the avocado
in half, remove the pit, and
scrape the flesh into a food
processor or blender.

4 Add the sour cream, lemon
juice, and salt and process
until smooth. Add the water and
process just to blend. If necessary,
add more water to thin the sauce.
Transfer to a bowl, taste and adjust
the seasoning, if necessary. Set
aside.

5 Preheat the grill. Heat a ridged
frying pan. Remove the
chicken from the marinade and
pat dry.

6 When the grill pan is hot, add
the chicken breasts and cook,
turning often, until they are
cooked through, about 10 minutes.

7 Meanwhile, arrange the tomato
halves, cut-sides up, on a
baking sheet and season lightly
with salt and pepper. Grill until hot
and bubbling, about 5 minutes.

8 To serve, place a chicken breast,
tomato half, and a dollop of
avocado sauce on each plate.
Sprinkle with coriander and serve.

VARIATION

To barbecue the chicken, light the
barbecue, and when the coals are
glowing red and covered with grey
ash, spread them in a single layer.
Set an oiled grill rack about 5
inches above the coals and cook
the chicken breasts until lightly
charred and cooked through,
about 15–20 minutes. Allow extra
olive oil for basting.

Chicken Sosaties with Curried Apricot Sauce

This is a South African version of kebabs, served with a delicious sweet-and-sour sauce spiced with curry powder.

INGREDIENTS

Serves 4

15ml/1 tbsp oil

1 onion, finely chopped

1 garlic clove, crushed

10 bay leaves

juice of 1 lemon

30ml/2 tbsp curry powder

60ml/4 tbsp apricot jam

60ml/4 tbsp apple juice

675g/1½lb skinless, boneless chicken
   breasts, cut into 2cm/¾in cubes

60ml/4 tbsp crème fraîche

salt

1 Heat the oil in a frying pan or saucepan. Add the onion, garlic and two of the bay leaves and cook over a low heat for 10 minutes, until the onions are soft. Add the lemon juice, curry powder, apricot jam and apple juice and season with salt. Cook gently for 5 minutes. Remove from the heat and set aside to cool.

2 Add the chicken to the marinade. Cover and set aside for 2 hours. Thread the chicken and the remaining bay leaves on to skewers and grill or barbecue for 6–8 minutes, turning often.

3 Simmer the marinade for 2 minutes. Stir in the crème fraîche and serve with the sosaties.

Spicy Indonesian Chicken Satay

This spicy marinade quickly gives an exotic flavour to tender chicken breasts. The satays can be cooked on a barbecue or under the grill.

INGREDIENTS

Serves 4

1 fresh red chilli, seeded and
   finely chopped

2 garlic cloves, crushed

60ml/4 tbsp dark soy sauce

20ml/4 tsp lemon juice or 15–20ml/
   3–4 tsp tamarind juice

30ml/2 tbsp hot water

4 skinless, boneless chicken breasts,
   about 175g/6oz each, cut into
   2.5cm/1in cubes

2 tbsp deep-fried onion slices

1 To make the marinade, mix together the chilli, garlic, soy sauce, lemon juice or tamarind juice and hot water in a bowl and set aside for 30 minutes.

2 Place the chicken in a bowl, add the marinade, mix well, cover and set aside for at least 1 hour. Tip the chicken and marinade into a strainer placed over a saucepan and leave to drain. Set the chicken aside.

3 Add 30ml/2 tbsp hot water to the marinade in the pan and bring to the boil. Lower the heat and simmer gently for about 2 minutes, then set aside to cool. When cool, add the onions.

4 Thread the chicken on to skewers and grill or barbecue for 10 minutes, turning regularly, until the chicken is golden brown and cooked through. Serve with the marinade as a dip.

Chicken with Herb and Ricotta Stuffing

These little chicken drumsticks are full of flavour and the stuffing and bacon help to keep them deliciously moist and tender.

INGREDIENTS

Serves 4

60ml/4 tbsp ricotta cheese

1 garlic clove, crushed

45ml/3 tbsp mixed chopped fresh herbs, such as chives, flat leaf parsley and mint

30ml/2 tbsp fresh brown breadcrumbs

8 chicken drumsticks

8 smoked streaky bacon slices

5ml/1 tsp wholegrain mustard

15ml/1 tbsp sunflower oil

salt and freshly ground black pepper

1 In a medium-size bowl, mix together the ricotta cheese, garlic, chopped fresh herbs and breadcrumbs. Season well with plenty of salt and pepper.

2 Carefully loosen the skin from each drumstick and spoon a little of the herb stuffing under it, smoothing the skin firmly into place over the stuffing.

3 Wrap a bacon slice tightly around the wide end of each drumstick, to hold the skin in place over the stuffing during the cooking time.

4 Mix together the mustard and oil and brush them over the chicken. Cook under a preheated medium-hot grill or on a barbecue for about 25 minutes or until cooked through, turning occasionally. Serve immediately.

Grilled Cashew Nut Chicken

This dish comes from the beautiful Indonesian island of Bali, where nuts are widely used as a base for sauces and marinades. Serve it with a green salad and a hot chilli dipping sauce.

INGREDIENTS

Serves 4

4 chicken legs
sliced radishes and ½ cucumber, sliced,
    to garnish
Chinese leaves, to serve

For the marinade

50g/2oz raw cashew or macadamia nuts
2 shallots or 1 small onion,
    finely chopped
2 garlic cloves, crushed
2 small red chillies, chopped
5cm/2in piece lemon grass
15ml/1 tbsp tamarind sauce
30ml/2 tbsp soy sauce
15ml/1 tbsp Thai fish sauce
10ml/2 tsp sugar
2.5ml/½ tsp salt
15ml/1 tbsp rice or white wine vinegar

1 Using a sharp kitchen knife, slash the chicken legs several times through to the bone. Chop off the knuckle end and discard.

2 To make the marinade, place the cashews or macadamia nuts in a food processor and process until fine. Alternatively, put the nuts in a mortar and grind them with a pestle.

3 Add the chopped shallots or onion, garlic, chillies and lemon grass and process thoroughly or mix well. Add the remaining marinade ingredients and process or mix well again.

4 Spread the marinade over the chicken and set aside in the refrigerator for up to 8 hours. Cook the chicken under a preheated grill or on a barbecue for 25 minutes, basting and turning occasionally. Garnish and serve on a bed of Chinese leaves.

Spatchcock of Poussins

Allow one poussin per person. Serve with boiled new potatoes and salad.

INGREDIENTS

Serves 4

4 poussins

50g/2oz/4 tbsp butter, melted

15ml/1 tbsp lemon juice

15ml/1 tbsp chopped mixed fresh herbs,
   e.g. rosemary and parsley, plus
   extra to garnish

salt and black pepper

lemon slices, to garnish

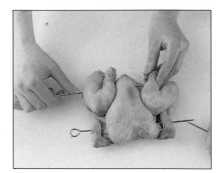

1 Remove any trussing strings and, using a pair of kitchen scissors, cut down on either side of the backbone and remove it. Lay the poussins flat and flatten with the help of a rolling pin or mallet.

2 Thread the legs and wings on to skewers to keep the poussins flat while they are cooking.

3 Brush both sides with melted butter and season with salt and pepper to taste. Sprinkle with lemon juice and herbs.

4 Preheat the grill to medium heat and cook skin-side first for 6 minutes until golden brown. Turn over, brush with butter and grill for a further 6–8 minutes or until cooked. Garnish with more chopped herbs and lemon slices.

Devilled Chicken

This spicy, barbecued chicken dish comes from southern Italy, where dried red chillies are a popular ingredient. Versions without the chillies are just as good.

INGREDIENTS

Serves 4

120ml/4fl oz/½ cup olive oil

finely grated rind and juice of 1 large lemon

2 garlic cloves, finely chopped

10ml/2 tsp finely chopped or crumbled dried red chillies

12 skinless, boneless chicken thighs, each cut into 3 or 4 pieces

salt and freshly ground black pepper

flat leaf parsley leaves, to garnish

lemon wedges, to serve

1 Make a marinade by mixing the oil, lemon rind and juice, garlic and chillies in a large, shallow glass or china dish. Add salt and pepper to taste. Whisk well, then add the chicken pieces, turning to coat with the marinade. Cover and marinate in the fridge for at least 4 hours, or preferably overnight.

2 When ready to cook, prepare the barbecue or preheat the grill and thread the chicken pieces on to eight oiled metal skewers. Cook on the barbecue or under a hot grill for 6–8 minutes, turning frequently, until tender. Garnish with parsley leaves and serve hot with lemon wedges for squeezing.

COOK'S TIP

Thread the chicken pieces spiral fashion on the skewers so they do not fall off during cooking. You can marinate and grill the lemon wedges with the chicken, if wished.

PIES &
PASTRIES

~

Old-fashioned Chicken Pie

The chicken can be roasted and the sauce prepared a day in advance. Leave to cool completely before covering with pastry and baking. Make into four individual pies if you prefer but bake for 10 minutes less.

Serves 4

1.5kg/3–3^{1}/2lb chicken

1 onion, quartered

1 sprig fresh tarragon or rosemary

25g/1oz/2 tbsp butter

115g/4oz/1^{1}/2 cups button mushrooms

30ml/2 tbsp plain flour

300ml/^{1}/2 pint/1^{1}/4 cups chicken stock

115g/4oz cooked ham, diced

30ml/2 tbsp chopped fresh parsley

450g/1lb ready-made puff or flaky pastry

1 egg, beaten

salt and black pepper

1 Preheat the oven to 200°C/ 400°F/Gas 6. Put the chicken into a casserole together with the quartered onion and the herbs. Add 300ml/^{1}/2 pint/1^{1}/4 cups water and season. Cover and roast for about 1^{1}/4 hours or until the chicken is tender.

2 Remove the chicken and strain the liquid into a measuring jug. Cool and remove any fat that settles on the surface. Make up to 300ml/^{1}/2 pint/1^{1}/4 cups with water and reserve for the sauce.

3 Remove the chicken from the bones and cut into large cubes. Melt the butter in a pan, add the mushrooms and cook for 2–3 minutes. Sprinkle in the flour and gradually blend in the stock.

4 Bring to the boil, season to taste and add the ham, chicken and parsley. Turn into a large pie dish and leave to cool.

5 Roll out the pastry on a lightly floured surface to 5cm/2in larger than the pie dish. Cut a narrow strip of pastry to place around the edge of the dish. Dampen with a little water and stick to the rim of the dish. Brush the strip with beaten egg.

6 Lay the pastry loosely over the pie, taking care not to stretch it. Press firmly on to the rim. Using a sharp knife, trim away the excess pastry and knock up the sides to encourage the pastry to rise. Crimp the edge neatly and cut a hole in the centre of the pie. This allows steam to escape during cooking. Decorate with pastry leaves and chill until ready to bake.

7 Brush the pastry with beaten egg (taking care not to glaze over the sides of the pastry). Bake in the oven for 35–45 minutes, until well risen and nicely browned all over.

Chicken, Cheese and Leek Jalousie

A jalousie is a family-size pastry roll with a mild creamy filling. Ready-made puff pastry and cooked chicken make this a good choice for informal entertaining.

Serves 6

1.5kg/3–3½lb roasted chicken
40g/1½oz/3 tbsp butter
2 large leeks, thinly sliced
2 garlic cloves, crushed
115g/4oz/½ cup button mushrooms, sliced
200g/7oz/scant 1 cup low-fat cream cheese
grated rind of 1 small lemon
45ml/3 tbsp chopped fresh parsley
2 x 250g/9oz packets puff pastry, thawed
 if frozen
1 egg, beaten
salt and freshly ground black pepper
fresh herbs, to garnish

1 Strip the meat from the chicken, discarding the skin and bones. Chop or shred the meat and set it aside.

2 Melt the butter in a frying pan over a low heat. Add the leeks and garlic and sauté for about 10 minutes. Stir in the mushrooms and cook for 5 minutes. Set aside to cool, then add the cream cheese, lemon rind, parsley and salt and pepper to taste. When completely cold, stir in the chicken.

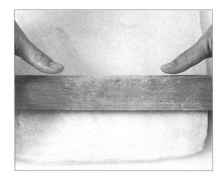

3 Stack the blocks of pastry on top of each other and roll out on a lightly floured work surface to a large rectangle about 35 x 25cm/ 14 x 10in. Lift the pastry with the rolling pin on to a non-stick baking sheet.

4 Spoon the filling on to the pastry, leaving a generous margin at the top and bottom and 10cm/4in on each side. Cut the pastry sides diagonally up to the filling at 2cm/¾in intervals.

5 Brush the edges of the pastry with the beaten egg. Draw the pastry strips over each other in alternate crosses to "plait" the pastry. Seal the top and bottom edges.

6 Glaze the jalousie with the beaten egg. Allow it to rest while you preheat the oven to 200°C/400°F/Gas 6. Bake for 15 minutes, then lower the oven temperature to 190°C/375°F/Gas 5 and bake for a further 15 minutes, or until the pastry is golden brown and crisp.

7 Allow the jalousie to stand for about 10 minutes before sliding it on to a board or platter to serve. Garnish with fresh herbs.

Kotopitta

This is based on a Greek chicken pie. Serve hot or cold with a typical Greek salad made from tomatoes, cucumber, onions and feta cheese.

Serves 4
275g/10oz filo pastry
30ml/2 tbsp olive oil
75g/3oz/^{1}/$_2$ cup chopped toasted
    almonds
30ml/2 tbsp milk

For the filling
15ml/1 tbsp olive oil
1 medium onion, finely chopped
1 garlic clove, crushed
450g/1lb cooked chicken, boned
50g/2oz/^{1}/$_4$ cup feta cheese,
    crumbled
2 eggs, beaten
15ml/1 tbsp chopped fresh parsley
15ml/1 tbsp chopped fresh coriander
15ml/1 tbsp chopped fresh mint
salt and black pepper

1 To make the filling, heat the oil in a large frying pan and cook the chopped onion gently until tender. Add the crushed garlic and cook for a further 2 minutes. Transfer to a bowl.

2 Remove the skin from the chicken and mince or chop finely. Add to the onion with the rest of the filling ingredients. Mix thoroughly and season with salt and freshly ground black pepper.

3 Preheat the oven to 190°C/ 375°F/Gas 5. Have a damp dish towel ready to keep the filo pastry covered at all times. You will need to work fast, as the pastry dries out very quickly when exposed to air. Unravel the pastry and cut the whole batch into a 30cm/12in square.

4 Taking half the sheets (cover the remainder), brush one sheet with a little olive oil, lay it on a well greased 1.35 litre/2^1/$_4$ pint ovenproof dish.

5 Sprinkle with a few almonds. Repeat with the other pastry sheets, overlapping them into the dish. Spoon in the filling and cover the pie in the same way with the rest of the overlapping pastry.

6 Fold in the edges and mark a diamond pattern on the surface with a sharp knife. Brush with milk and sprinkle on any remaining almonds. Bake for 20–30 minutes or until golden.

Chicken and Ham Pie

This domed double-crust pie is suitable for a cold buffet, for picnics or any packed meals.

INGREDIENTS

Serves 8

400g/14oz ready-made shortcrust
    pastry
800g/1³/₄ lb chicken breasts
350g/12oz uncooked gammon
about 60ml/2fl oz/¹/₄ cup double cream
6 spring onions, finely chopped
15ml/1 tbsp chopped fresh tarragon
10ml/2 tsp chopped fresh thyme
grated rind and juice of ¹/₂ large lemon
5ml/1 tsp freshly ground mace
salt and black pepper
beaten egg or milk, to glaze

1 Preheat the oven to 190°C/
375°F/Gas 5. Roll out one-third of the pastry and use it to line a 20cm/8in pie tin 4cm/1¹/₂in deep. Place on a baking sheet.

2 Mince 115g/4oz of the chicken with the gammon, then mix with the cream, spring onions, herbs, lemon rind, 15ml/1 tbsp of the lemon juice and the seasoning to make a soft mixture; add more cream if necessary.

3 Cut the remaining chicken into 1cm/¹/₂in pieces and mix with the remaining lemon juice, the mace and seasoning.

4 Make a layer of one-third of the gammon mixture in the pastry base, cover with half the chopped chicken, then add another layer of one-third of the gammon. Add all the remaining chicken followed by the remaining gammon mixture.

5 Dampen the edges of the pastry base. Roll out the remaining two-thirds of the pastry to make a lid for the pie.

6 Use the trimmings to make a lattice decoration. Make a small hole in the centre of the pie, brush the top with beaten egg or milk, then bake for about 20 minutes. Reduce the oven temperature to 160°C/325°F/Gas 3 and bake for a further 1–1¹/₄ hours; cover the top with foil if the pastry becomes too brown. Transfer the pie to a wire rack and leave to cool.

Chicken en Croûte

Chicken breasts, layered with herbs and orange-flavoured stuffing and wrapped in light puff pastry, make an impressive dish to serve at a dinner party.

Serves 8

450g/1lb packet puff pastry
4 large chicken breasts, boned and skinned
1 egg, beaten

For the stuffing

115g/4oz/1 cup leeks, thinly sliced
50g/2oz/1/3 cup streaky bacon, chopped
25g/1oz/2 tbsp butter
115g/4oz/2 cups fresh white breadcrumbs
30ml/2 tbsp chopped fresh herbs, e.g.
    parsley, thyme, marjoram and chives
grated rind of 1 large orange
1 egg, beaten
salt and black pepper

1 To make the stuffing, cook the sliced leeks and bacon in the butter until soft. Put the breadcrumbs into a bowl with the mixed herbs and plenty of seasoning. Add the leeks, bacon and butter with the grated orange rind and bind together with the beaten egg. If the mixture is too dry and crumbly, you can stir in a little orange juice or chicken stock to bring it to a moist consistency.

2 Roll the pastry out to a large rectangle 30 x 40cm/12 x 16in. Trim the edges and reserve for decorating the top.

3 Place the chicken breasts between two pieces of clear film and flatten to a thickness of 5mm/1/4in with a rolling pin. Spread a third of the leek stuffing over the centre of the pastry. Lay two chicken breasts side-by-side on top of the stuffing. Cover the chicken breasts with another third of the stuffing, then repeat with the remaining chicken breasts and the rest of the stuffing.

4 Make a cut diagonally from each corner of the pastry to the chicken. Brush the pastry with beaten egg.

5 Bring up the sides and overlap them slightly. Trim away any excess pastry before folding the ends over like a parcel. Turn over on to a greased baking tray, so that the joins are underneath. Shape neatly and trim any excess pastry.

6 With a sharp knife, lightly criss-cross the pastry into a diamond pattern. Brush with beaten egg and cut leaves from the trimmings to decorate the top. Bake at 200°C/400°F/Gas 6 for 50–60 minutes or until well risen and golden brown on top.

Chicken Parcels with Herb Butter

A herb-coated, buttery chicken fillet wrapped up in crisp pastry.

INGREDIENTS

Serves 4

4 chicken breast fillets, skinned

150g/5oz/³/4 cup butter, softened

90ml/6 tbsp chopped mixed fresh herbs, such as thyme, parsley, oregano and rosemary

5ml/1 tsp lemon juice

5 large sheets filo pastry, defrosted if frozen

1 egg, beaten

30ml/2 tbsp grated Parmesan cheese

salt and black pepper

1 Season the chicken fillets and fry in 25g/1oz/2 tbsp of the butter to seal and brown lightly. Allow to cool.

2 Preheat the oven to 190°C/ 375°F/Gas 5. Put the remaining butter, the herbs, lemon juice and seasoning in a food processor and process until smooth. Melt half the herb butter.

3 Take one sheet of filo pastry and brush with herb butter. Cover the rest of the pastry with a damp dish towel. Fold the pastry sheet in half and brush again with butter. Place a chicken fillet about 2.5cm/1in from the top end.

4 Dot the chicken with a quarter of the remaining herb butter. Fold in the sides of the pastry, then roll up to enclose it completely. Place seam-side down on a lightly greased baking sheet. Repeat with the other chicken fillets.

5 Brush the filo parcels with beaten egg. Cut the last sheet of filo into strips, then scrunch and arrange on top. Brush the parcels once again with the egg glaze, then sprinkle with Parmesan cheese. Bake for about 35–40 minutes, until golden brown. Serve hot.

Chicken and Stilton Pies

These individual chicken and Stilton pies are wrapped in a crisp, shortcrust pastry and shaped into pasties. They are great for lunch, served hot or cold.

Makes 4

350g/12oz/3 cups self-raising flour

2.5ml/^{1}/2 tsp salt

75g/3oz/6 tbsp lard

75g/3oz/6 tbsp butter

60–75ml/4–5 tbsp cold water

beaten egg, to glaze

For the filling

450g/1lb chicken thighs, boned and
    skinned

25g/1oz/^{1}/4 cup chopped walnuts

25g/1oz spring onions, sliced

50g/2oz/^{1}/2 cup Stilton, crumbled

25g/1oz celery, finely chopped

2.5ml/^{1}/2 tsp dried thyme

salt and black pepper

3 Remove any fat from the chicken thighs and cut into small cubes. Mix with the chopped walnuts, spring onions, Stilton, celery, thyme and seasoning and divide the filling equally among the four pastry circles.

4 Brush the edge of the pastry with beaten egg and fold over, pinching and crimping the edges together well. Place on a greased baking sheet and bake in the oven for about 45 minutes, or until golden brown.

1 Preheat the oven to 200°C/400°F/Gas 6. Mix the flour and salt in a bowl. Rub in the lard and butter with your fingers until the mixture resembles fine bread-crumbs. Using a knife to cut and stir, mix in the cold water to form a stiff, pliable dough.

2 Turn out on to a work surface and knead lightly until smooth. Divide into four and roll out each piece to a thickness of 5mm/^{1}/4in. Cut into a 20cm/8in circle.

Chicken and Game Pie

A rich filling of chicken and dark meat, spiced with ginger.

INGREDIENTS

Serves 4

450g/1lb boneless chicken and game meat
(plus the carcasses and bones)
1 small onion, halved
2 bay leaves
2 carrots, halved
a few black peppercorns
15ml/1 tbsp oil
75g/3oz streaky bacon pieces, rinded and
chopped
15ml/1 tbsp plain flour
45ml/3 tbsp sweet sherry or Madeira
10ml/2 tsp ground ginger
grated rind and juice of $^1/_2$ orange
350g/12oz ready-made puff pastry
beaten egg or milk, to glaze
salt and black pepper

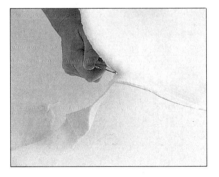

1 Place the carcasses and bones in a pan, with any giblets and half the onion, the bay leaves, carrots and black peppercorns. Cover with water and bring to the boil. Simmer until reduced to about 300ml/$^1/_2$ pint/1$^1/_4$ cups, then strain the stock, ready to use.

2 Cut the chicken and game meat into even-size pieces. Chop, then fry the remaining onion in the oil until softened. Then add the bacon and meat and fry quickly to seal. Sprinkle on the flour and stir until beginning to brown. Gradually add the stock, stirring as it thickens, then add the sherry or Madeira, ginger, orange rind and juice, and seasoning. Simmer for 20 minutes.

3 Transfer to a 900ml/1$^1/_2$ pints/ 3$^3/_4$ cups pie dish and allow to cool slightly. Use a pie funnel to help hold up the pastry.

4 Preheat the oven to 220°C/425°F/Gas 7. Roll out the pastry to 2.5cm/1in larger than the dish. Cut off a 1cm/$^1/_2$in strip all round. Dampen the rim of the dish and press on the strip of pastry. Dampen again and then lift the pastry carefully over the pie, sealing the edges well at the rim. Trim off the excess pastry, use to decorate the top, then brush the pie with egg or milk.

5 Bake for 15 minutes, then reduce the oven temperature to 190°C/375°F/Gas 5, for a further 25–30 minutes.

Chicken Charter Pie

Since this dish comes from Cornwall, rich double cream is used in the filling.

Serves 4

50g/2oz/4 tbsp butter

4 chicken legs

1 onion, finely chopped

150ml/^{1}/4 pint/^{2}/3 cup milk

150ml/^{1}/4 pint/^{2}/3 cup soured cream

4 spring onions, quartered

20g/^{3}/4 oz fresh parsley, finely
   chopped

225g/8oz ready-made puff pastry

120ml/4fl oz/^{1}/2 cup double cream

2 eggs, beaten, plus extra for glazing

salt and black pepper

1 Melt the butter in a heavy-based, shallow pan, then brown the chicken legs. Transfer them on to a plate.

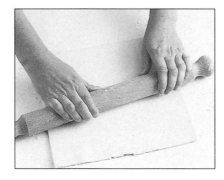

2 Add the chopped onion to the pan and cook until softened but not browned. Stir the milk, soured cream, spring onions, parsley and seasoning into the pan, bring to the boil, then simmer for a couple of minutes.

3 Return the chicken to the pan with any juices, then cover tightly and cook very gently for about 30 minutes. Transfer the chicken and sauce mixture to a 1.2 litre/2 pints/5 cups pie dish and leave to cool.

4 Meanwhile, roll out the pastry until about 2cm/^{3}/4in larger all round than the top of the pie dish. Leave the pastry to relax while the chicken is cooling.

5 Preheat the oven to 220°C/425°F/Gas 7. Cut off a narrow strip around the edge of the pastry, then place the strip on the edge of the pie dish. Moisten the strip, then cover the dish with the pastry. Press the edges together.

6 Make a hole in the centre of the pastry and insert a small funnel of foil. Brush the pastry with egg, then bake for 15–20 minutes.

7 Reduce the oven temperature to 180°C/350°F/Gas 4. Mix the double cream and eggs, then pour into the pie through the funnel. Shake the pie to distribute the cream, then return to the oven for 5–10 minutes. Remove from the oven and leave in a warm place for 5–10 minutes before serving, or cool completely if serving cold.

Chicken Bouche

A spectacular centrepiece, this light pastry case contains a delicious chicken and mushroom filling with a hint of fruit. Ideal served with freshly cooked vegetables.

INGREDIENTS

Serves 4

450g/1lb ready-made puff pastry

beaten egg, to glaze

For the filling

15ml/1 tbsp oil

450g/1lb/3 cups minced chicken

25g/1oz/4 tbsp plain flour

150ml/^{1}/4 pint/^{2}/3 cup milk

150ml/^{1}/4 pint/^{2}/3 cup chicken
    stock

4 spring onions, chopped

25g/1oz/^{1}/4 cup redcurrants

75g/3oz button mushrooms, sliced

15ml/1 tbsp chopped fresh
    tarragon

salt and black pepper

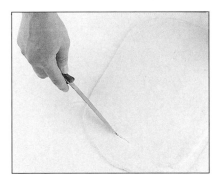

1 Preheat the oven to 200°C/ 400°F/Gas 6. Roll half the pastry out on a lightly floured work surface to a 25cm/10in oval. Roll out the remainder to an oval of the same size and draw a smaller 20cm/8in oval in the centre.

2 Brush the edge of the first pastry shape with the beaten egg and place the smaller oval on top. Place on a dampened baking sheet and bake for 30 minutes.

3 For the filling, heat the oil in a large pan. Fry the minced chicken for 5 minutes. Add the flour and cook for a further 1 minute. Stir in the milk and stock and bring to the boil.

4 Add the spring onions, redcurrants and mushrooms. Cook for 20 minutes.

5 Stir in the fresh tarragon and season to taste.

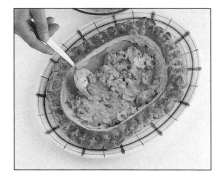

6 Place the pastry bouche on a serving plate, remove the oval centre and spoon in the filling. Place the oval lid on top. Serve with freshly cooked vegetables.

VARIATION

You can also use shortcrust pastry for this dish and cook as a traditional chicken pie.

Index